Nourishing Love

In *Nourishing Love*, Murray Bodo has provided a literary banquet of foods for reflection, inspiration, and instruction. For all who seek to develop a deeper personal appreciation of Mary's centrality in Catholic faith and spirituality, here is food for mind and heart. A variety of resources—teachings, reflections, poetry, traditional prayers—will serve those who preach and who direct spiritual exercises and retreats. Ensconced within the poetic meditations on Mary's life are a number of "teaching moments" in which Bodo offers clear summaries of complex theological traditions. His articulation of the theology of the Incarnation developed by John Duns Scotus is a gem. This book is the fruit of a lifetime of searching for the elusive but essential truth behind the words we pray when we address this woman of ancient Palestine with the words, "Holy Mary, Mother of God."

— MARGARET CARNEY, OSF

In *Nourishing Love*, Fr. Murray Bodo draws readers into a series of captivating reflections and poetry about the Blessed Mother. This is a perfect book for those looking to expand their appreciation for the Franciscan spiritual tradition, as well as for those who desire to deepen their Marian devotion. Those already familiar with Fr. Murray's creative writing style will recognize his distinctive poetic voice in each line, while those who have yet to encounter his wonderful work will find a welcome introduction to his inspired writing and spiritual guidance in this book.

— DANIEL P. HORAN, OFM, Duns Scotus Chair of Spirituality, Catholic Theological Union and author of *God is Not Fair and Other Reasons for Gratitude*

Nourishing Love

· · · · · · · · · · ·

A Franciscan
Celebration of
MARY

Murray Bodo, OFM

franciscan
media®
Cincinnati, Ohio

Scripture citations are taken from the *New Revised Standard Version Bible,* copyright ©1989 by the Division of Christian Education of the National Council of Churches of Christ in the U.S.A. and used by permission. Unless otherwise indicated, quotations from the writings of St. Francis are the author's translation. Unpublished English translation from "The Process of Canonization of St. Clare" was done by Frances Teresa Downing, OSC. Excerpt from *Living Things* copyright © 2006 by Anne Porter. Reprinted with permission from Steerforth Press.

Library of Congress Cataloging-in-Publication Data
Names: Bodo, Murray, author.
Title: Nourishing love : a Franciscan celebration of Mary / Murray Bodo, OFM.
Description: Cincinnati, Ohio : Franciscan Media, [2021] | Summary: "St. Francis had a deep and lifelong devotion to Mary, the Mother of God, committing his order to her care. Franciscan Murray Bodo explores that relationship in this evocative and deeply spiritual encounter with Marian devotion across the centuries"—Provided by publisher.
Identifiers: LCCN 2021000560 (print) | LCCN 2021000561 (ebook) | ISBN 9781632533340 acid free paper) | ISBN 9781632533357 (ebook)
Subjects: LCSH: Mary, Blessed Virgin, Saint–Devotion to. | Franciscans–Spiritual life.
Classification: LCC BX2160.23 .B63 2021 (print) | LCC BX2160.23 (ebook) | DDC 232.91–dc23
LC record available at https://lccn.loc.gov/2021000560
LC ebook record available at https://lccn.loc.gov/2021000561

Cover and book design by Mark Sullivan
Cover image by Holly Schapker
Copyright ©2021, Murray Bodo, OFM. All rights reserved.

ISBN 978-1-63253-334-0

Published by Franciscan Media
28 W. Liberty St.
Cincinnati, OH 45202
www.FranciscanMedia.org

Printed in the United States of America.
Printed on acid-free paper.
21 22 23 24 25   5 4 3 2 1

To the memory of my mother, Polly Bodo,
whose devotion to Mary I hold dear;

To Susan Saint Sing, whose home in Stuart, Florida was spared
in Hurricane Dorian through the intercession of Mary;

To Wendy Buhl, whose last words to me
when she was dying were, "What about Mary?"
This is what I know, Wendy,
and what I wish I'd had time to say;

And to Our Lady of Loreto,
who welcomed me into her home.

Contents

Foreword

This book clearly emerges from the accumulated reflections of many years. Fr. Murray Bodo draws on his own spiritual journey and places what he has learned beside his intuitions about Mary, the Mother of the Lord. To these he has added some of the poems that have studded his way and shone on the whole the light he has gained from the Franciscan theologian John Duns Scotus. For many centuries it has been a common practice to seek insight about our own Christian growth through reflection on the lives of others who have gone before us and who have impressed us. This quest has drawn on spiritual reading and Scripture to help us in following the advice of the writer of the Letter to the Hebrews, who encourages us to think of our spiritual forebears and to "reflect on the outcome of their lives" (Hebrews 13:7) as a way to a deeper understanding of our own lives and outcomes.

A renewal of interest in the Ignatian Spiritual Exercises in recent years has encouraged people to use their imagination as a means to prayer, to read the narratives of Scripture as a doorway into the deeper meaning of their own experiences, and to see themselves in an unfolding salvation history. As we gain insight into God's dealings with humanity we grow in our understanding and, hopefully, become agents in our own lives rather than victims or simply survivors. Fr. Murray, like most of us, has had moments when surviving seemed all he could do, but he also offers us some recollections in tranquility in which even "mere survival" begins to take its place as an essential aspect of growth.

What is less common, though equally valid, is to reverse the direction of flow. Instead of looking to Scripture for help in understanding ourselves, we look at ourselves and what we have learned about life for insight into the important people in our story. They were human beings like us and the broad patterns of human maturing do not seem to have changed much over the centuries. It is very enlightening to reflect on the great figures of salvation history in the light of our own story. This is what we do spontaneously with our friends, family and neighbors, but we are often more diffident in extending the process to our spiritual family and forebears.

Here Fr. Murray shares his thoughts on Our Lady and his relationship with her within the context of his own journey of growth and the development of his own warm humanity. With rich support from Franciscan theology, he uses his own story as the basis for approaching the mind and heart of Mary in the last years of her life. We journey with her as she grows older in Ephesus, living in the house of John, the Beloved Disciple. We watch her, at the end of her life, coming to understand ever more fully all that had happened earlier. We journey with her as she approaches death with all that must have meant to her. With her, we learn to share a degree of transformation whereby the diminishments of age and the narrow doorway of death open onto the vast plains of infinite love, experienced even now.

Most of us have some pivotal incidents to which we can look back and say it was *that* moment, *that* encounter, *that* incident that was a defining moment in our lives. For Mary, in Fr. Murray's interpretation, that first great defining moment was the annunciation by the angel Gabriel. What was new to me—and both surprising and interesting—was the suggestion that in one sense the visitation of Gabriel to Mary was an event of such power that it began explosively but never really ended. It brought with it that eternity from which the angel came. Through the angel's visit, another dimension permanently intruded into her life and all life. It opened a way for her to begin learning what it meant that her Son was both God and man. Gabriel thus became a continuing and catalytic presence in her life. The irruption of eternity irreversibly changed her sublunary world into an exploration of eternity. Through this first annunciation, she was led further and further into light, into the many different kinds of light by which we see or by which we are blinded.

In these intuited reflections, John, the Beloved Disciple, is also a presence, drifting in and out of this woman's awareness like someone drifting in and out of the room, peacefully and supportively. He is aware of her, of her needs, and even more of the immense inner spaces through which she is traveling. She does not come across as an old woman looking back on life, so much as a mature and ripened human being coming every day to a richer and deeper understanding of eternal events in which she had been (and was still) a pivotal player. These two perceptions come together very poignantly in the poem "Madonna Pietá," in which the ongoing Incarnation in the womb of Mary is balanced by the ongoing desolation of humanity "lying heavy, broken, in your open lap."

The author's scholarship, intuition, and imagination are shown clearly not only in the meditations on Mary but as the author himself looks back on all that had gone before in the light of all that came later. Just as the annunciation was operative throughout

Mary's life, so for most of us the early events of our more ordinary lives remain operative through the years. The result is rather like looking for a long time at a portrait of someone we knew well and realizing that the artist's intuition has both challenged and enriched our understanding. There was more to it than we had noticed. In the process it is almost as if we, too, share a journey through the redemption of humanity. Let us hope our suffering planet also still journeys with us toward wholeness and happiness.

—Frances Teresa Downing, OSC

Introduction

The infinite possibilities of the virgin soul of Mary. She is what medieval theologians called a coincidence of opposites, a seeming conjunction of opposite realities: a fruitful virgin, the one St. Francis calls, "Virgin made church." She is a virgin who gives birth to the Church: first, to Christ the Head, and then, to the Mystical Body of Christ, which is the communion of those born again in Christ.

In Mary, virginity is not a kind of prideful badge of honor, a selfish barrenness and self-absorption. But rather her virginity becomes, instead, infinite fruitfulness. She continues to give birth to the ever-expanding Body of Christ, which is the Church. That is the essence of Mary: a divinely graced virgin who becomes the mother of all.

What gratitude this evokes in the human soul! Someone, a mere girl, says yes to the soul of the universe: the Incarnation of God as a baby born to a virgin, a baby whose progenitor is the very Spirit of God, the Holy Spirit, who is the love of the Father and the Son, a love so intense that it becomes one of the Persons of the Blessed Trinity. It is this Person, the Holy Spirit, who overshadows the Virgin Mary so that she gives birth to Incarnate Love made flesh. Through Mary, God is born among us as one of us to be the image and the very enfleshment of Eternal Love: Jesus the Christ. He is the firstborn of countless children born of Mary through Baptism in the same Spirit who overshadowed Mary and made her our mother. Indeed, as St. Francis said more simply and clearly, "She is Virgin made Church."

The pages that follow are her story as a human being who brings God to earth, Mary of Nazareth, the human mother of Jesus, who becomes the Queen of Heaven and Earth, the Mediatrix of All Graces.

The writing in this book comprises three different genres: meditations, poems, and reflections. The meditations come from a Franciscan way of praying that the scholar Ewert Cousins called "the mysticism of the historical event," which consists of taking a scene from Scripture and putting yourself into the scene, imagining you are one of the characters, and letting the scene open itself up to you. It is not just an intellectual exercise. It is a dimension of prayer in which you are open to grace and to the spiritual energy that derives from that particular scene or event in Scripture. It is akin to a pilgrimage to a geographical place where an extraordinary spiritual event took place. The pilgrims who make their way there don't just seek an intellectual experience of the event but pray that the grace of that particular place will be given them to live it out in their life that day and every subsequent day of their lives. St. Ignatius of Loyola later embraced this Franciscan way of praying, and it became an integral part of his *Spiritual Exercises.*

The meditations here are focused on the last year of Mary's life when she is living with John, the Beloved Disciple, in Ephesus. (It's possible she may also have lived for a time with John on Patmos.) It was Jesus himself who gave them to each other as mother and son when he spoke to them from the cross thus: "When Jesus saw his mother and the disciple whom he loved standing beside her, he said, 'Woman, here is your son.' Then he said to the disciple, 'Here is your mother.' And from that hour the disciple took her into his home" (John 19:26-28).

The poems here are a collection of my poems about Mary from the time I was an adolescent boy to the present, again revealing how the imagination works as a knowing faculty of the mind and heart, revealing to us in the imagining what we did not know we knew.

Finally, the reflections explore the meaning of Mary: who she is both in the theology and tradition of the Church and, more specifically, who she is in Franciscan theology and prayer. All of this, together with prayers I have appended at the end of the book, I envision as a kind of Franciscan Mary Miscellany, a collection of writings that strive to do homage to the Blessed Virgin Mary whom St. Francis made the Advocate and Protectress of the Franciscan Order, under the title of Our Lady of the Angels.

The Story of Mary

We know very little of Mary, the mother of Jesus, from Sacred Scripture, the oldest reference being circa 57 A.D. in St. Paul's Letter to the Galatians. Paul writes that "when the fullness of time had come, God sent his Son, born of a woman" (Galatians 4:4). No name is given to the "woman." There are a couple of references in Mark's Gospel, as well: "Then his mother and his brothers came…" (Mark 3:31). And again, "Is this not the carpenter, the son of Mary…?" (Mark 6:3).

In the Gospel of John, Mary is present at the Wedding Feast at Cana: "And the mother of Jesus was there" (John 2:1). The only other reference to Mary in John's Gospel is at the Crucifixion: "Meanwhile, standing near the cross of Jesus were his mother, and his mother's sister, Mary the wife of Clopas, and Mary Magdalene" (John 19:25). And finally, The Acts of the Apostles records that Mary is with the Apostles in the room where they were praying after the Ascension of Jesus. They were all gathered "together with certain women, including Mary the mother of Jesus… (Acts 1:14).

This leaves us with the Gospels of Matthew and Luke. Most of what we know of Mary from the New Testament is from the infancy narratives of these two Gospels, which were written more than eighty years after the events they describe concerning the birth and boyhood of Jesus. These narratives, coming so long after Jesus's birth, take on an almost myth-like nature. They are the results of some eighty years of an oral tradition whose stories were told from storyteller to storyteller to storyteller, growing in the telling and in the imagination of those who heard the stories and passed them on. It was left to the stories' divinely inspired scribes—the Apostle Matthew, and Luke, the physician and companion of St. Paul—to give the stories a written form. Luke, the most literary of the Evangelists, also wrote the Acts of the Apostles.

Luke, especially, brings to the foreground Mary, the one always in the background, the one whose name was "mother" or "woman." It is hard to believe how close-up in the foreground Mary has emerged over the centuries. The image that comes to mind is that of a new rosebud tightly closed during the time of Jesus's life among us. Jesus was the center of both the Holy Family and of the family that became the Church, that gathering of believers formed into a coherent entity. It was Jesus who had to be proclaimed first and foremost, Jesus whose mystery as God and a human being was to be probed first by the extraordinary thinker and theologian, St. Paul, and whose life was to be told by the four Evangelists: Matthew, Mark, Luke, and John. It was Jesus who was to be defined by the early councils of the Church.

Meanwhile in the garden of the new Eden a closed, tightly hidden rosebud grew quietly, slowly, imperceptibly. Then in the fullness of time Jesus was at last more understood and proclaimed to be "one Lord Jesus Christ, the Only begotten Son of God, born of the Father before all ages. God from God, Light from Light, true God from true God, begotten, not made, consubstantial with the Father; through him all things were made. For us and for our salvation he came down from heaven, and by the Holy Spirit was incarnate by the Virgin Mary, and became man" (Nicene Creed).

When all that was defined, and Jesus Christ was beginning to be understood in his fullness, then the petals of the rosebud that was Mary began to unfold and open to the faithful in their faith and liturgies, their devotion and prayer, all of which is what the Catholic Church calls Tradition.

Mary was being meditated upon and written about in relation to her role in salvation history by the Fathers of the Church, by Church councils, and by papal documents that defined doctrines and dogmas of the Church that grappled with what it means that God's Son had a human mother. And Mary then began to be defined in reference to the mystery of the Incarnation. Theologians, saints, and mystics began to ask, Who was she who was chosen to be God's mother? Is she different from other mothers? When she leaves this earth, does she have a special place and role in God's kingdom and in the new heaven and the new earth proclaimed in the book of Revelation?

Questions pile on questions about the woman who was Jesus's mother until she becomes the Mystical Rose, the ever opening mystery of her Divine Motherhood that reaches its apogee in the Middle Ages and Renaissance. Cathedrals are built in her honor, artists paint her over and over again, poets write of her, musicians sing her praises, and the infancy stories of Matthew and Luke fire the imaginations of playwrights and liturgists and composers. And all the while the cult of Mary is growing so that faithful Christians implore her intercession whom they consider to be above all the saints and angels who intercede or are intermediaries for us.

All of this extraordinary growth of devotion to Mary stems from the tidings the Angel Gabriel brought to Mary, especially in that dramatic scene at the beginning of the Gospel of Luke, which begins with an annunciation by an angel of the Lord to the priest Zachary that his barren, aging wife Elizabeth "will bear you a son and you will name him John." And "he will be great in the sight of the Lord…and will turn many of the people of Israel to the Lord their God…to make ready a people prepared for the Lord" (Luke 1:5–17).

And Elizabeth did indeed conceive. Then in the sixth month of her pregnancy, "the Angel Gabriel was sent by God to a town of Galilee called Nazareth, to a virgin engaged to a man whose name was Joseph, of the house of David. The virgin's name was Mary" (Luke 1:26–28).

Of all the stories I've read in my lifetime, few opening lines move me more than those two sentences of Luke. I know now what's coming, of course, but there was, once upon a time, a young boy in a New Mexico border town who opened the Douay Rheims version of the New Testament and read those words for the first time, and began to fall in love with story itself as the vehicle of grace and knowledge. We are not just our minds. We live and move and have our being in and with the world around us. We experience our lives through all of our senses, and all of that experience is conveyed in story, which is more than ideas and beliefs. Story has movement and sound, and portrays how we interact with our environment, with humans and all living things, from plants to animals to the landscape of our lives in time.

A story follows someone around, asking questions like, Where did he/she come from? Who are they? Where are they going? What is keeping them from getting there? What is going to happen to them? That whole gestalt is what story addresses, using those kinds of questions and then answering them through the same five senses by which we experience life, our own life. And story takes place in time, that mysterious dimension that begins, whether it is stated or not, with, "Once upon a time...."

So, *once upon a time, there was a young Jewish girl who lived in a town named Nazareth. She was a virgin, and her name was Mary, and it happened once that an angel appeared to her and told her that she was full of grace and was going to conceive a child. She was to name him Jesus, and he would be called the Son of the Most High.* Now how is that for a beginning? All kinds of questions pop into the reader's or listener's mind, even though it is rather matter-of-factly told in the third person, omniscient point of view.

Or the story could begin like this: *I am Gabriel, the archangel. I come from heaven where I live forever in the presence of God. "Don't be afraid, Mary. I come in peace and love from the God of Abraham and Moses, who has a message for you, 'Hail, favored one. The Lord is with you, for you have found favor with God. You will conceive in your womb and bear a son, and you will name him Jesus.'"* Same story, different point of view, different questions. And all kinds of possibilities open up for a dialogue between Mary and the Angel.

Or, it could be Mary's story, the story she tells. *It all began one day as I was sitting and spinning wool for a shawl I was making for my mother, Ann. There was nothing special about the day until, hearing a whooshing sound, I was startled to look up and see before me a winged man, beautiful and powerful and full of light, and he was bowing before me and saying, almost chanting, "Greetings, favored one! The Lord is with you!"*

I wondered, could he be talking to me? But he was staring intently at me, and I was suddenly afraid, not knowing what the greeting meant or what I was supposed to say. But he immediately calmed me with his sweet voice, "Do not be afraid, Mary, for you have found favor with God." How did he know my name? And what did it mean that I had found favor with God? Again a different point of view with lots of possibilities for getting into Mary's mind and heart as she grappled with what was happening to her on an ordinary day that had suddenly turned magical and other worldly.

Story. That is the great gift the Scriptures give us in the infancy narratives of Matthew and Luke. And it is those stories and a few other short vignettes in the Gospels of Mark and John that form the basis of what we call mariology, the study of the theology that derives from the story of Mary and her son Jesus. And her son Jesus was and is the reason, the root, and the complementarity that makes her story complete.

The story of Mary is the story of Jesus; his story is the completion of hers, and hers the completion of his. That complementarity of Man and Woman continues the story of the Garden of Eden and takes it in a wholly different direction. For example, it is not to a man that God sends his offer of a new covenant, but to a woman. Mary is the new Abraham, being the virgin mother of a people more numerous than the stars. And it all begins when she gives birth to the Son of God. Their story, Jesus's and Mary's, from the moment Mary says yes to God's invitation to give birth to Jesus, is masculine and feminine, Yin and Yang, Animus and Anima. The new covenant is their story, not just Jesus's story, and from that eternal union derives the story and the theological implications of the Blessed Virgin Mary in the history of the New Covenant, recorded originally in what we call "The New Testament of Our

Lord and Savior Jesus Christ." That is why we lift up our hearts and pray, as Christians have prayed for centuries,

Hail Mary, full of Grace,
the Lord is with you.
Blessed are you among women,
and blessed is the fruit of your womb, Jesus.

Holy Mary, Mother of God,
pray for us sinners, now
and at the hour of our death. Amen.

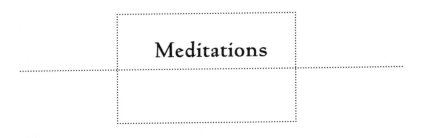

Meditations

SCENES FROM THE LIFE OF MARY

"It is impossible to put oneself in the place of another human being, to imagine seeing the world through his or her eyes, and to clothe those thoughts with language without presuming—but this is what artists are called to do, and do it we must with conviction, devotion, and humility. We can never truly know another soul. But love compels us to try."

—Angela Alaimo O'Donnell, *Andalusian Hours*

Light

It was the light she remembered. Even now, in all this darkness that attends aging, it is the light she remembers. The light. It is without horizons and yet most of the time it seems just beyond the horizon, the invisible presence that though it is inside her, is just beyond the horizon she became when the Holy Spirit overshadowed her. It is her hope, this light, especially in the deepest night. The memory of it now as then, just after the angel's light, the words like the static of lightning disappearing and light remaining like a gentle rain falling, the room as quiet as before, the silence returning as light.

The closeness of the dark night. The memory of yesterday's dawn making the dark light, the light dark, all because of that other Light out of the invisible, the place of the angel's arrival and departure.

She is breathing softly now. The memory calms, strengthens, assures that the memory is of a real thing, that extraordinary annunciation, the baby beginning to light up what she'd thought was a dark place within her, the darkness of the invisible now made visible inside her. That is what is real, that memory of light. And everything since then has been the light coming and going in the visible world that was her life with a son named Jesus, who came and stayed and left, in and out of the ordinary day and night of their lives, she and Joseph and the small light in and out of the invisible, the small light that was her son Jesus, growing, becoming the Christ with and without her who was and is the hidden one, and she the mother of the ordinary light becoming the Light that was to come, did come, and will come into the world.

These are her thoughts now as she waits here in the home she and John have made here in Ephesus. She waits, as she did as a young girl, waits in prayer and silence, for what good news another angel of God might bring her of God's son and hers, now reigning as the Light of the Universe.

She and John are both dreamers, and they share their reveries. She was given to John and John to her by the Light who seemed to be in the darkness but not of it when he said as he hung dying on a rough-hewn cross, "Woman, here is your son," and to John, his beloved disciple, "Here is your mother." She knew somehow not to be afraid of this new message because the Light was in the words, and she said in reply, as she had in Gabriel's first annunciation, "Be it done to me according to your word."

She knew in her heart that in embracing this new son, she was not losing the son who seemed to be dying. For the Light shone brightly within her as when she said yes to his conception in her womb.

She knew that some new good news was about to happen, as it did indeed in his rising from the dead, the son she thought had died. And this new son, John? It was he who brought her and the disciples confirmation of the news of the empty tomb as they watched in prayer in the upper room.

John and Peter rushed into the room, and John looked at her as Peter announced the good news she already knew when the light flooded her whole being earlier that morning when Mary Magdalen told them she had seen the Lord. And so she had.

And so they all would see him that very night when the Risen Jesus, the child of her womb, entered the room, though the doors were closed, and said, "Peace be with you," and showed them his wounds, and breathed on them, saying, "Receive the Holy Spirit." And her Spouse, the Holy Spirit, once again filled her whole being as when she conceived Jesus in her womb.

That was a long time ago now, and she felt, just remembering everything that happened, that she was slowly dying into her own thoughts that one day would become an eternal reality and she would suddenly see the heaven of what was already as close to her as her very skin, though she could not see what she knew was there to be revealed when the Father, her Son, and the Holy Spirit would open heaven to her.

In the meantime, she would tend to this home in Ephesus and to John and to the disciples here who visit them almost daily telling stories of new disciples, of healings, of the power of their words when the Holy Spirit is upon them.

Nazareth

He said he was an angel, one of those who stand before the throne of God. He was sent, he said, by God, a messenger from the throne of the Most High God. He told her not to be afraid.

And she was not afraid because his message was good news: God was with her; she had found favor with God and would conceive in her womb and bear a son, and she was to name him Jesus.

She is remembering now what she has stored up in her heart all these years. It began the first time she experienced the Light that is God. It dwelled inside the angel's words, "The Holy Spirit will come upon you and the power of the Most High will overshadow you" (Luke 1:35). That is what happened in the very moment of the angel's speaking. And she embraced the light that was the words themselves. She said yes to so beautiful a proposal, its light, its love. And she said simply that she was God's handmaid. May it be done to her according to God's word spoken by the angel. And the Light then filled her whole being. And the angel left her alone with the light illumining her womb.

She is tiring now. The immensity of the memories. The light. It is enough for today. Now she will just rest in the light. She will choose when to return to reverie again. She will know when. She will find the thoughts, not they her.

John

"You look tired, Mary."

It is John, his shadow falling at her feet as he stands in the doorway, the setting sun just above the horizon. How strong he looks, how full of energy and sparkling words. Sparkling. How strange, yet accurate, that the sight of him should summon that word into her mind. John of the Sparkling Words. Sparkling. Like his whole being, though he thinks such deep thoughts and sees such visions, terrifying at times. And when they are terrifying, he is silent, lost in his own thoughts, though he smiles if he happens upon her or comes home after a seemingly long time away.

"I was thinking and remembering."

"You do, indeed, look so. Lost in the past as I, recently, am lost in the future."

"Today, the future must look good, as Jesus promised it would be. You are smiling more than usual."

"Yes. Good. I saw you today, your future and ours, we who live in the Light."

"How strangely different we are, dear John. I have no visions. I have already seen with my own eyes, as have you, but you are given visions now to transcribe in words for those who will come after you. My thoughts are memories mostly. They come every day, like the one today of a boy standing by his father reverently holding a piece of wood and asking, 'How does this wood connect to other pieces of wood, father, and how do two pieces of wood become a crossbeam to hold up a house?'

"Those kinds of thoughts preoccupy me, John, thoughts that are memories I've held in my heart for years."

"Yes. You are our memory trove. Only you have the memories no one else has now. I, on the other hand, live now not only remembering but somehow dwelling in the visions given me by that same boy whom I knew as an extraordinary man and prophet who, we both know, is and was the Son of God…. Am I tiring you, mother Mary?"

"It is a good tiring when we speak of him who now has become someone other than when he was here with us, talking, learning, waiting to be shown when his ministry to others might begin."

"Yes, mother Mary, he is someone other now, but as we both know, he is also who he always was even before he came into your blessed womb. He belongs now to everything and everyone in heaven and earth."

"And they belong to him."

"And that is what my visions seem to be all about, the future that began when he ascended into heaven. As he sent then the Holy Spirit to be with us, so in the future he himself will come."

"As you told me, John, when you said you saw the future in visions when we were living in Patmos."

"And now I am writing them down, my hand directed by God's Holy Spirit upon me. I write only when I, as you were, am visited by his angel and am overshadowed by God's Holy Spirit."

John's Gospel

She was gazing out the window when John came through the doorway; and when she turned at the sound of his footstep, she saw that, as often, he was filled with light. A softer light than usual, it felt to her like a healing balm. And as always, she felt no darkness in John. In him and through him light overcame the darkness because in him was the Christ, her son Jesus, in whom is all light.

She smiled as soon as he turned toward her.

"You look tired, John. You've been gone a long time today."

"I am tired, but it does not matter. I was out in blinding sun in an arid place letting the sun sear me and writing of that other John, your cousin they call the Baptizer. How fierce he was, how caked with sand and dry like the desert he lived in. How powerful his utterance."

"He was his father's son, the strict priest Zachary who lived every jot and tittle of the law, so unlike my gentle son Jesus."

"True. And John lived in his own inner world. He did not even recognize Jesus for who he was until the Holy Spirit descended on Jesus as John was baptizing him in the Jordan.

"And today I was writing how it was with John and Jesus. As Jesus himself told you, John was power, the power of light over darkness. It was that power that was behind the power of his preaching."

"Yes. John the Baptist was himself a light, as you and I are, John. We both have lived in the light that is Jesus, and we recognize that light in others, as I did in you when you walked through the open door. It is a light not of our doing, but of his."

John remained silent. She knew he was thinking about what she said. It was the way with her and John. Silence was a comfortable communication beyond words, especially when something important had been spoken—as when she had said, "It is his doing, not ours."

And it was so now. John was rehearsing in his mind the words he would write in the morning. They would complete the prologue of his Gospel: "From his fullness we have all received, grace upon grace. The law indeed was given through Moses; grace and truth came through Jesus Christ. No one has ever seen God. It is God the only Son, who is close to the Father's heart, who has made him known" (John 1:16–18).

John continued to stand in quiet repose, in awe of the God who had given him these words, especially the last two sentences he'd not intended to say. They seem to have just come of their own and attached themselves to what he was rehearsing in his mind. They were grace, the "grace upon grace," which was all he'd intended to say. How mysterious words were. They had at times their own life and led him where they willed. They took him further into what he was trying to say. They were of God, as light was, and as he and Mary were.

Then, as if coming from a far place in his mind, he turned gently to Mary and said, "I see you've made our supper, Mary, the barley bread and herbs, and the fish I caught for us this morning—and figs!"

"Yes, the figs! They are a gift from the synagogue disciples in Ephesus."

"How kind of them. I know them, of course, from when they sent us the lovely squash and lentils last week, and I went to the synagogue to thank them."

"I know they are your favorite! And Jesus, too, as you know, loved figs. And I wasn't pleased when you told me how he had cursed the barren fig tree."

"Sons! They do grow away from us, don't they, mother Mary?"

"Yes, it is the way with children and parents. And I do know that he was enacting, as you put it, a parable of the Jewish people. But Jesus just sounded like a spoiled child when I first heard from you what he had done. It was so unlike him. But I am glad he spoke more tenderly to the fig tree later when he used it to illustrate another truth he wanted us to know."

"You mean about learning from the fig tree?"

"Yes, when he said, 'From the fig tree learn its lesson: as soon as its branch becomes tender and puts forth its leaves, you know that summer is near' (Mark 13:28).

"That sounds more like Jesus, doesn't it? The other story sounded to me at the time more like something his firebrand cousin would say and do."

And so the evening went as they continued till dark talking and praying and ending the day in silence and sleep.

Gabriel

....

She knew from the moment of the rush of Gabriel's wings and his lilting, "Hail, full of Grace," that she was only the handmaid, the servant of the Most High God, and Gabriel only the messenger of God's message. But what she could not have known was that she was more than God's servant; she, mysteriously, was to be a vessel of the living God, and she was afraid. And Gabriel knew she was afraid and said, "Do not be afraid, Mary, for he who will be born of you will be known as the son of God."

How can this be, she thought, and immediately she knew that God had come to her because she was a woman, she was pure potential for motherhood, and no one human would be the agent. And knowing, Gabriel said, "Yes, Mary, God the Holy Spirit will overshadow you, and of that Divine Power you will conceive the son of God." Then she, in turn, replied, "Let it be with me according to your word" (Luke 1:38). And that was it, Gabriel himself open-eyed at her response; he himself, like her, unaware of the depths of the words they were exchanging, aware though of whose words Gabriel had announced to her. The words' unfolding would be her pregnancy full of grace and light unimaginable: a child whom she was to name Jesus, a child of her womb, a son whose origins were in eternity begotten of God, born of a woman who was her very self, a mere girl who was suddenly woman, mother of a boy who was pure mystery though he was somehow in her like any baby and would come from her into the world.

That is how she remembered it, here in Ephesus. She was now as she was then: a girl, a woman, waiting and watching for the angel who would announce the word of her passing into the heaven where her Son ruled at the right hand of the Father. She was not afraid. She needed no Gabriel to reassure her. She'd lived too long in the immensity of the mystery to doubt.

Nor did she wonder who she would be in eternity. She would be who she always was: Mary, the mother of God's Son. She suspected that would be her role for all eternity: mother, woman, the completion of the love of the mysterious faces of God—Father, Son, Holy Spirit—the mystery moving through the three of them into her, visible in eternity as it is invisible on earth.

She would share these thoughts with John, who would see immediately that they are not her own aged self-absorption but her meditations on God's mystery, her part in which was only as great or as small as God's plan, God's word. And the Word, as John insists, was there in the beginning and became flesh through her only because God chose to reveal the Word by becoming human, by enfleshing the Word in Jesus.

How marvelous such thoughts were! How sustaining when she remembered how Jesus suffered and died and she helpless to do anything to save him who was saving her and the whole of the Father's creation by hiding his divinity in suffering and dying like a mere man. How much was still hidden from her. How much will be revealed when Jesus comes for her and leads her into the mystery of who he and she really are, when the mystery is opened and revealed, when the human Jesus becomes the eternal Word he always was, even as a child in her womb and as a dead man in a tomb.

She smiled at how much she still remembered, the girl who thought and prayed and played in Nazareth. The Little Thinker, her mother called her. *Who we are we were,* she thought. *And when I die, will I just die into my thoughts that will bring me into heaven on the arm of my son?*

John's Vision

John realizes she is not just a tool, a means for God to become human. She is herself a feminine force in the cosmos of his visions, a complementarity whose presence will reveal itself more and more once Mary lies down with her forefathers and foremothers in death. She, like her son, will not die to die; she will die to live forever in the Trinity of Persons who chose her to bear Christ in time. She will merge with the Word and its eternal speaking. She will be God's eternal choosing of male and female together, willed by the Father, embraced by God's Spirit, birthing mother of the Son throughout eternity, revealing the humanity of God to humanity.

She herself will appear again and again in time. In and out of eternity. She will be the new ark of the covenant, the eternal enfleshing of the Son of God. When she appears again among us, she will ever be the place of God's presence among us, the place where Jesus is the eternal Christ, the human dwelling place of God.

But now she is here with me; she is Jesus's mother dying. Even in dying she is revealing what will never die, the eternal Word spoken in and through her womb. And where she is and where she appears among us, there will be her Eternal Spouse and Her Son.

For now she is his adopted mother Mary with whom he eats and talks as she awaits the transformation that is life and death and death and life until the final coming of Jesus, the Christ who is ever her son. That is *the* revelation of all his revelations as he prays and ministers to the brothers and sisters of Jesus in Ephesus, the brothers and sisters who have heard the Word and are living it out in Ephesus and everywhere the Word is heard and lived. And as he prays and writes and serves, so Mary prays and sings over and over her Song of the Annunciation:

> My soul magnifies the Lord,
>   and my spirit rejoices in God my Savior
> for he has looked with favor
>   on the lowliness of his servant.
> Surely from now on all generations
>   will call me blessed;
> for the Mighty One has done great
>   things for me,
>   and holy is his name.
> His mercy is for those who fear him
>   from generation to generation.
> He has shown strength with his arm;
>   he has scattered the proud in
>   the thoughts of their hearts.
> He has brought down the powerful
>   from their thrones,
>   and lifted up the lowly;
> he has filled the hungry
>   with good things
> and sent the rich away empty.
> He has helped his servant Israel,
>   in remembrance of his mercy,
> according to the promise he made to
>   our ancestors,
>   to Abraham and to his descendants forever.

This is the song she sings to those who visit her here. This is her ministry to the brothers and sisters of Jesus. She is his remembrance and ever will be.

Transfiguration

She did not recognize him at first. He had the look of someone who has been away many years in a far-off land and has come back changed into someone other than the one we knew. And what a change was there. The radiance was almost unbearable until he spoke what seemed a single word, "Peace be with you." For it was the word *peace* that broke the spell as Jesus stood there showing them his side and hands, the wounds as radiant as he was from the journey he had made through death to the house where they, the disciples, were gathered.

She wondered now when it was she had begun to include herself among the disciples. Was Jesus's appearance after his resurrection from the dead the first time she realized she was one of the disciples of her own son?

Or was it when Jesus, dying on the cross, had given her John as her son? However and whenever it was, she now was in the presence of the Lord and she, his mother, was one of his disciples. And now here standing before them was a new Jesus, a man reborn in death into Christ the Lord, the Son of God in the flesh. Her flesh, yes, but transformed now into someone more who always dwelled within him. Would they all be transformed like this in death? Would each be someone more who was always within but in death revealed to all with eyes to see what they have become?

John speaks often of this when they sit around the hearth fire and talk. He talks of the miracle of transfiguration that happened when Jesus led Peter, James, and John himself up a high mountain to pray. But he would not write of that experience. He said Jesus told them to tell no one of what they had seen and heard until he had been raised from the dead. But John said his whole Gospel is the revelation of the glory of God in the signs Jesus worked for all the people and not a select few. For John the transfiguration is evident in all the signs Jesus worked and also in the last discourse of Jesus at the Last Supper for those who had ears to hear.

Peter, as is his wont, has begun to tell the story; and it will, John says, be written down by Mark, Peter's disciple, and by the garrulous Matthew, and no doubt also by the physician Luke, who comes to her often and asks for stories of Jesus's birth and childhood and how it was that she came to be his mother.

But he, John, will not record the story he has told her about how Jesus led him and Peter and James up a high mountain where Jesus was transfigured before them, how his clothes became dazzling white, how Elijah and Moses appeared to them talking with Jesus, and how a cloud overshadowed them and a voice from the cloud said, "This is my Son, the Beloved, listen to him," and then how all the glory disappeared and they were again with the Jesus who walked up the mountain with them.

This happened six days after Jesus had told the disciples of his death and rising from the dead and foretold that there were some standing there who would not taste death until they had seen that the kingdom of God had come in power. For John those who were in the room when the risen Jesus entered and showed them the glory of his risen body and his glorious wounds were given the sign that the kingdom of God had, indeed, come in power.

In John's mind, to have told the story of Jesus's transfiguration on Mount Tabor would have diminished the extraordinary experience, which John believes cannot be told and heard. It has to be seen and lived. "Let others tell the story," John says. "I will concentrate on transfiguration stories of those other than a chosen few, stories of the many who know who Jesus is because they took personally and lived out Jesus's words, 'They who have my commandments and keep them are those who love me; and those who love me will be loved by my Father, and I will love them and reveal myself to them'(John 14:21)." That, John says, is everyone's transfiguration story.

Annunciations

She looks at the corner of the room near the door and sees Gabriel there. She sees him often, this angel of her annunciation. He seems never to change, as she has over the years, but looks the way he looked on that graced day when she, a young girl, heard the rush of wings and saw before her the terrifying image who is the Archangel Gabriel, and he was telling her not to be afraid. He had tidings of joy for all the people and for her, in particular, for she was to bear and give birth to a baby who would be called the Son of the Most High.

How great was that telling that she had meditated on ever since. And usually when she is meditating, Gabriel reappears, saying nothing but his presence reassuring her that she is not to be afraid. Even in the terrible passion and death of Jesus, Gabriel visited her, and that time he did speak, reassuring her with Jesus's own words that she is not to be afraid, for "you will have pain, but your pain will turn into joy. When a woman is in labor, she has pain because her hour has come. But when her child is born, she no longer remembers the anguish because of the joy of having brought a human being into the world. So you have pain now; but I will see you again, and your hearts will rejoice, and no one will take your joy from you" (John 16:20–23)

Now as she grows feebler, her angelic visitations seem more frequent, as if Gabriel were preparing her for something further she is to know and that he will announce in due time. Every day she is with Jesus in prayer, her Son now glorified and transparent of Divinity as he was not when he was growing up and living with her and Joseph in Nazareth.

The Storyteller

Mary knows him well enough now that she expects him to come through the door telling a story. And so it happens, more often than not. And she knows his favorite stories because he's beginning to repeat himself, apologetically asking her if he's already told the story he goes and tells her anyway.

The story he now tells again and again is of how Jesus cures the man born blind. It is one of the favorites that seems to preoccupy him. It's about seeing, even though you are blind, and being blind even though you can see. There is seeing and there is seeing. The difference is the light by which you see.

He tells Mary that Jesus gave him, especially on the mountain of the transfiguration, another light to see by, the kind of light the Pharisees in the story don't have, though the blind man did have. The blind man saw that Jesus is of God, and that seeing was more important than the seeing of one who sees with ordinary light, like the light of fire or the light of the sun. This new light enables one to see beyond what you can see with your ordinary eyes and ordinary light. The Pharisees see that the blind man can see, but they can't see that other dimension that the healed man sees: that Jesus is of God.

Every time he tells the story to Mary, he fills in new little details, as storytellers do. She said yesterday's story was her favorite so far.

There once was a blind beggar who everyone said was a real "character" with a quick, sarcastic tongue. Then one day as we were walking along, Jesus saw the blind beggar and decided he would make of him an example of what real seeing is. And so, as I knew someone would, one of the disciples asked, "Did this bitter man sin or was it his parents, that he was born blind?"

"Neither," Jesus said. "He was born blind so that God's works will be revealed in him. And I now must do that work while it is still day, for the night is coming on when no one can work. I am the light of the world as long as I am here in the world."

Then Jesus did an astonishing thing. He called the blind man to him and spat on the ground and made mud with his saliva and spread mud on the man's eyes, saying to him, "Go wash in the pool of Siloam." So the man did and came back jumping and gesticulating and looking at everything and everyone with wonder, for he was now able to see.

Now what was astounding was not the healing or asking the man to wash in the pool of Siloam, but the way Jesus healed him, spitting on the ground and making mud and spreading it on the man's eyes. We asked ourselves why Jesus did that. But others, of course, were all taken up with the healing, however it happened. They were saying things like, "Isn't this the man who used to sit and beg, bemoaning his fate?" Or, "No, that's not the man; he just looks like him." But the man himself kept insisting, "I am the one who was the blind beggar you're talking about."

This caused one in the crowd to ask, "Then how were your eyes opened so that you can now see."

"It was the man called Jesus. He made mud and spread it on my eyes and said, 'Now go to Siloam and wash.'"

It seems the man himself was impressed with Jesus making mud and spreading it on his eyes. This must be very important to the story somehow. But the manner of the healing went right over the questioner's head, and he said, "So where is this Jesus now?"

"I don't know."

Then, of course, the whole story got detoured because Pharisees were there and all they heard was that Jesus healed the man on the sabbath.

"That," John said, "is how the Word is proven to have been made flesh. There are human stories about the incarnate God. And the stories themselves become a further embodiment of the Word made flesh, the Word who lived among us as a human." And then he added, "It is the making of mud that distinguishes this story. Why would Jesus heal in that manner?"

He then told Mary how honored she is in this gesture by Jesus, her son. He said that Jesus was emphasizing that the Word did indeed become flesh, did become human, using a kind of poultice made of human saliva and the earth as a vehicle for the healing of the man born blind. It is also an image of God forming Adam from the dust of the very earth he would then walk upon and be buried in. Christ the new Adam and a new image of God. He would walk upon the earth as the son of Mary, revealing in sacramental signs that he was also the Son of God. Jesus made of mud a kind of sign, as he will later make of bread and wine, *the* sign of God's presence among us. And only those whose eyes are opened by the Incarnation of God in Jesus can see God in the smallest gesture of Jesus while he lived among us. And Mary is once again gently reminded that she partook of all those gestures for thirty years of intimacy with the God who would, at the age of thirty, begin to reveal to others what she witnessed for so many years: Intimacy with Jesus is intimacy with God.

What Is Remembered

John says she's starting to live more and more in her memories. And how should she not? They are the contours of her life since the very first memory of Gabriel and his astonishing words, "Greetings, favored one! The Lord is with you" (Luke 1:28) Then her cousin Elizabeth echoes Gabriel's words with, "Blessed are you among women" (Luke 1:42).

John says that these are the memories that color every other memory of hers. And how should they not? For everything truly of God in her life has flowed from Gabriel's first words spoken with such power and from the words that followed, all stored up from eternity: "Do not be afraid for you have found favor with God. And now you will conceive in your womb and bear a son, and you will name him Jesus. He will be great and will be called the Son of the Most High, and the Lord God will give to him the throne of his ancestor David. He will reign over the house of Jacob forever, and of his kingdom there will be no end" (Luke 1:30-34).

And how should she not have those words fixed in her memory forever—to the amazement of the disciple, the physician Luke, that she should know them by heart? For we often remember well and long what we committed to memory when we were young, as she was in her annunciation by an angel of the kingdom of God.

It overpowered all other visitations, like, for example, the visitation of the Magi, the wise men from the East who came to Bethlehem to see and do homage to her newborn son. She was neither amazed nor frightened when they arrived, for they were of this world, while Gabriel was of the kingdom of heaven, sent not by a star but by God as God's messenger to a young girl in Nazareth.

But she does see both Gabriel and the Magi vividly in her reverie. The color of the clothes the Magi wore, those yellows and greens and reds, and the gold and damask trimmings. And the beauty of Gabriel, his striking eyes and the melodious sound of his voice. For the voice, too, adds color to life, its lilt and timbre. But what made Gabriel special and terrifying was magnitude, the light and aura of his presence that never seemed at rest but continued to vibrate, even when he himself was no longer moving, like music struck from a gong like the one the Magi's servant carried. Like the heavens telling the glory of God, did Gabriel's very presence tell of the movement and song of the heavens. And it was not a nervous vibrating, but a beautiful movement and sound, as if the whole of the heavens and earth were moving and he within them.

She wanted to sing and dance. She thought of Miriam, Moses's sister, who took up the timbrel and began to dance for joy, along with the women of Israel, when Pharaoh's army were drowned by the returning waves of the Red Sea. Except, there was something triumphant, almost warlike, in Miriam's music and dance, and the song of Gabriel was that of those who surround God with their music, their whole being moving and singing with the heavens themselves.

So it was not just the message that drew Mary to remember again and again the annunciation of Gabriel. It was his song and movement which were from the unseen heavens where God dwelt with God's Son who, when he entered her womb, sang his own song and brought his own movement that she could feel as she carried Jesus daily as he grew into the baby born in Bethlehem, looking like all other babies, no glory surrounding him as God's glory surrounded and shone from the Archangel Gabriel. All the amplitude of Gabriel's astounding voice and movement was now but a newborn human baby lying in a little crib of ordinary straw. Somewhere inside that little bundle of baby was the magnitude and amplitude of God's own Son that was not revealed, as far as she knew, until Jesus was transfigured on the mountain in the presence of Peter, James, and John. And that only briefly, a fore-taste of Jesus's resurrection and ascension into heaven a couple of years later.

On the mountain the ordinary became extraordinary, as in the annunciation and birth of Jesus, the extraordinary became the ordinary. It seemed to her an image of all their lives once they had received the baptism of water and the Spirit. Ordinary water led to a supernatural grandeur within that lies hidden in an ordinary human being, until the coming of Jesus, the Christ, when the ordinary will shine and sound the magnitude and amplitude of the transfigured human being.

John has been saying much of the same to her during the last few months, confirming and prophesying in images powerful in their own magnitude of what is to come when the new heaven and the new earth have come to pass. How consoling that is, how full of a peace beyond her understanding. She remembers and thinks such thoughts when she lays her head upon the rug where sleep comes easily and she breathes to a rhythm already inside her that one day will be revealed as the breath of God breathing her.

The Glance of Love

This time of year, the time of Passover, the days felt heavier, even now so many years after Jesus was betrayed by that poor, unfortunate man, Judas. She had forgiven him almost immediately but more powerfully on that glorious day when the Holy Spirit once again overshadowed her, this time in the upper room where she and the disciples were praying in anticipation of the visitation of the Holy Spirit, which Jesus had promised them before he ascended into heaven. In that same Spirit who came to her in the conception of Jesus she knew that her forgiveness of Judas was real, and though the days seemed heavier when she thought of that kiss of Judas in the Garden of Gethsemane, she did indeed forgive him. And even though she was free of any resentment toward Judas, the days still seemed heavy because of Judas's end and the pain that must have caused Jesus.

She felt heavy this time of the year for Jesus, too. How much he suffered, how deep was his pain and sense of abandonment during his harrowing passion and death. And even though now he was gloriously reigning as the Christ, the Lord of the Universe, his passage to that glory was so fraught with pain and agony that the memory of it still lingered within her. How dark are the passages that lead to light, how painful the sting of death that leads to life eternal! And all of that passage deserved remembrance as did the passage from slavery to the freedom of the Hebrew people released from their bondage in Egypt but still having to make the difficult, painful journey through the desert to the Promised Land.

Simeon prophesied that a sword would pierce her own soul, and so it did very early in the life of Jesus when Joseph and she learned that Herod was killing all the first-born children two years of age and younger who lived in and around Bethlehem.

Herod thought Jesus was a threat to his throne because of the wise men from the East who asked Herod where the newborn child, the king of the Jews, was to be born. And when the chief priests and the scribes told Herod and the wise men that the child would be born in Bethlehem of Judea, Herod sent the wise men there, asking them to return and tell him where this child lived so that he, too, could go and pay him homage. But being warned in a dream, the wise men did not return to Herod but went home by another road. When Herod realized what had happened, he fell into a rage and ordered the murder of all children who were two years old or younger in and around Bethlehem.

Joseph and she, because of Joseph being warned in a dream what Herod was doing, were already on their way to Egypt when the slaughter of the children was being carried out. She mourned them and their devastated parents for a long time, even after she and Joseph and Jesus returned from Egypt. The frequency of her times of mourning lessened; but the memory, when it returned, remained fresh and the wound in her heart raw.

They did not return to the land of Israel because of the fear of Herod's son, Archelaus. They went back instead to Galilee, to their town of Nazareth, where the angel Gabriel had first appeared to her and told her that she was to be the mother of a baby who would be known as the Son of God.

All those disruptions and sufferings were redeemed and trans-figured when she remembered the suffering of Jesus when he was condemned to death, then tortured before carrying his cross of crucifixion to Calvary. Meeting him in the street in Jerusalem broke her heart so that she could feel the sword piercing her heart repeatedly, almost killing her when she stood beneath the cross and saw her son die the excruciating death of a common criminal.

But what could have killed her, did not because of what happened when she met Jesus as he carried his cross to Calvary. It was simply a look. She will never forget that glance of love in Jesus's eyes when she looked into his battered and bloody face as he stood stooped over from the weight of the cross. She saw clearly in a flash of light that he was dying for love. And that memory, she knew, must be *the* memory of his passion and death. That, she told herself, is the memory to hold on to, even after suffering and death is no more.

From that memory, she knew not to dwell on the suffering and pain, the deaths and dyings of our lives; she knew to dwell on the love with which one suffers and dies. She saw it in her son's eyes. She suddenly knew that Jesus was already rising; she saw it in the glance of unbelievable love in the eyes that looked at her. From that moment on, even as Jesus continued on his way, carrying his cross, and as he fell and was stripped of his garments and nailed to the cross, she only saw the love in his eyes. *That is how he saved us*, she thought, *not by the horror of his passion and death, but by the love that shone in his eyes.*

From that moment on, she would have to remind herself whenever she would remember and start to dwell on Jesus's suffering, that love redeemed it all, and with the coming of the Holy Spirit on Pentecost, she again saw in a flash of light that love was the reason from all eternity. Jesus came to love us and show us the love of the Father and how we are to love the Father.

And with that vision, there seemed no past anymore, or even future. Everything was now, everything was new and exciting in the present. And how marvelous to live in that reality that was a preview of what was to come but more importantly, was already here, happening in her. She was living in the kingdom and all that needed to happen was that moment when she entered and saw the kingdom of love that was already there inside and all around her.

Though that realization seemed harder to hold on to now that she was getting older and the heavy days seemed to come around more quickly when once upon a time Jesus suffered and she suffered with him. It seemed harder not to move into the memory of his suffering and to forget the glance of love. She had to remind herself more often to embrace the memory and move on as she had been able to do so easily immediately after and for all the years following the descent of the Holy Spirit upon her and the other disciples.

But even now, as in this moment of reverie, if she were to begin to lose her focus, she has learned to turn most naturally to the Psalms; it is a wholly natural turn of mind and attention. And beginning to recite them, sometimes aloud even if John was not there, she moved from memory to the present moment.

So now she turns to the sacred texts she has held in her mind by the same memory that had briefly engaged her again of past hurts and suffering until she remembered that look of love. She pulls up the words as naturally as she would begin talking to John,

O come, let us sing to the Lord;
let us make a joyful noise to the rock of our salvation!

Let us come into his presence with thanksgiving;
  let us make a joyful noise to him with songs of praise! (Psalm
95)

Already she is beginning to sing the words that pour out of her as
she chants,

O sing to the Lord a new song,
  for he has done marvelous things.
He has remembered his steadfast love and faithfulness
  to the house of Israel.
Sing praises to the Lord with the lyre,
  with the lyre and the sound of melody.
With trumpets and the sound of the horn
  make a joyful noise before the King the Lord. (Psalm 98)

Suddenly she is dancing, her old feet shuffling across the earthen
floor, her whole body keeping time to her chant, her arms waving,
hips moving to a new music within her, deep music from the fullness of her heart, from her joy as she pauses and raises her arms
to heaven singing,

For the Lord is good;
his steadfast love endures forever,
and his faithfulness to all generations. (Psalm 100)

Tears of joy are running down her cheeks as she continues
humming and John is standing in the doorway smiling and
Gabriel has moved forward from his place in the corner, his wings
trembling to the music.

The Prayer of Waiting

She did not recognize him at first, though she knew it was he. His eyes were the same, the color of the sea, hazel brown to green depending on the light and season of the year. "Little pools," she called them when he was a baby. Yet how changed his countenance and body now. What marvels of transformation between dying and rising!

She could only imagine what had transpired between his death on the cross and this extraordinary man standing in the room, the doors locked and they all gathered in prayer, and she wondering how and when he would reappear among them, and would he still be her son? But, of course, he was, and he called her "our mother." It was the "our" that was new and sounded prophetic, sounded almost eternal. A given, something that was there from eternity.

The other disciples only looked on, wondering. He had no discernible clothes, though he was covered in an opaque aura, a sort of raiment that allowed his glorified wounds to reveal that skin was still there. His hands hung out from the tunic-like raiment, and his feet, though bare, touched the floor the way they did when he would come in from playing and would remove his sandals, as though the earthen floor were sacred, and he needed to feel it as he walked over to embrace her.

How she had waited for that embrace! Her whole life from the time Gabriel, God's messenger, appeared to her, she has lived her life in waiting. She waited in Egypt for God to reveal that she and Joseph and Jesus would be safe to return to their homeland. Even now she waited, doing what she always did in her daily life, a lesson she had learned when she was told of her cousin Elizabeth's pregnancy. She had made the extraordinary journey to Elizabeth who was in her sixth month of waiting as she held John the Baptizer within her womb, both she and Elizabeth waiting then to be acted upon by God. Each of them was wondering what mystery would be revealed in the child she bore. Waiting. Waiting for the mystery to be revealed to them. Waiting and doing what all women did in the waiting, namely, living as they always did, only now for the babies as well as themselves. In her and Elizabeth, they already knew, were boys, whose tiny feet would one day walk upon the earthen floor that their extraordinary lives would transcend when, as men, they would begin the redemption of Israel.

All life, it seemed to her, was shown us in the waiting of a woman's pregnancy. You lived from day to day, as before, but ever aware that there was a miracle within waiting to reveal itself. The difference for Elizabeth and Mary herself was that they both already knew that their children would be extraordinary in the history of their people. It had nothing to do with them but with God's working quietly within them. And yet, it had everything to do with them, for their child would be blood of their blood, flesh of their flesh, so they themselves would be bearing the child in the reverence of prayer, the awareness like unto their own deep prayer. And it was that prayer that made the waiting itself a prayer, and that their very way of being and doing would be one part of their contribution to the forming of the child within them.

They could not force the time to be shortened, they could not act in some grand way with the gestures reserved for their sons.

But each in her own way had prepared their sons by the love with which they surrounded this child-to-be in their waiting for him to be revealed. They waited to see how their love had made a very baby in whose eyes they would see their own love given prayerfully for nine months.

And now in this new rebirth of Jesus, Mary could still see her own love in the eyes that looked back at her as he walked upon the earthen floor, much as he had walked the first time he waddled and stumbled into her arms, a little baby boy becoming. She had held Jesus in her arms once he'd walked so determined but hesitantly toward her open arms; she had held him lifeless in her lap when he was taken down from the cross; she would now wait for him to embrace her with the love with which she had embraced him all the days of his life. Even when he left home to embrace the Father's will that he preach and teach, suffer and die for the people of Israel, she embraced him lovingly in her heart every day as she waited for the next mystery to be revealed. *When God works upon us*, she thought, *then the real working of our lives is in the waiting, waiting to receive what is given us when we wait upon the Lord in all we are and all we have.*

What new waiting will now follow upon this new embrace of him who approaches her God-like in his bearing and in his walk but still walking like an ordinary man upon the earthen floor upon which he was born.

A Nourishing Presence

John can feel Mary's presence or absence in the house, even before he enters, so tangible is the spiritual force that emanates from her whole being. Of all the disciples of Jesus, hers is the most tangible aura of goodness and spiritual power. And yet, she is the most retiring and quiet of all. Never does she put herself forward and do wondrous things that would put her in the center. Always it is Jesus she radiates, always it is the other, like John himself, that she builds up and encourages. She is the hearth that makes the house they share full of warmth and goodness. She is the constant reminder of Jesus, the God-man she bore in her womb, the man who lived with her for thirty years.

She has shared with Luke how it was before and after the birth of Jesus, but only the events that were meant to be shared with the whole people, like the events foretold by the prophets, but how it was in the home she never speaks of. He wonders often how they lived together she and Jesus—and Joseph when he was still on earth. But John can surmise, just from the way she is with him.

The first thing he noticed when she came to live with him after Jesus's crucifixion, was the way she inhabited their space together. The house itself, within and without, was suffused with her presence, not in any way that would seem that she was taking charge or taking over the space. In fact, she was almost invisible at times, even when she was there in the room. It was as though the place they inhabited together was somehow cleansed and purified by a humble presence, a peace that made the house holy, that made him not notice the passing of time when they were there together.

And so it has remained. These days when he returns, they talk and eat together; and always it is mostly of him they talk, his day, his reflections on how the kingdom of God is growing in Ephesus, how new disciples are being added almost daily to those who believe and are baptized in water and the Spirit. And she listens intently, as she must have to Jesus and Joseph, their strong male influence filling the house whose listening walls and floors both absorbed and gave back to them the peaceful aura of her presence there.

It is the way Mary listens that makes him and others feel important, their lives, their thoughts, their plans and doings. He always feels expanded when he and Mary talk. There is an authority in her without being authoritarian. It is, John feels, a sympathy, a compassion, that gives authority to what he writes of Jesus's story. She is always there, though she's never mentioned, except to relate what she herself has related to him as one of the signs that Jesus is the Son of God. The story of the Wedding Feast of Cana is one of the clearest examples.

She and Jesus are at the marriage feast which, in itself, is the kind of thing that happened throughout their lives together, and no one thought to mention it as part of the history of salvation. They were guests among guests. And then came this particular wedding where their hosts ran out of wine.

It is Mary who notices, and when she tells Jesus they have run out of wine, he wonders what that has to do with him. It would seem a snub to someone other than Mary, who is listening to what he is not saying, namely, that the beginning of the signs he is to show forth couldn't be about making sure there was wine for the guests at a wedding feast, could it? But Mary, who has spent her life listening to the word of God, knows that it is, that changing water to wine is in fact *the* sign of the beginning of the kingdom on earth: water to wine to make special marriage itself, to elevate the ordinary to the extraordinary.

Mary is the handmaid of the Lord God. She is obedient, submissive, faithful; she listens with a pure and humble spirit. But she is more than the handmaid of God; she is the mother of Jesus, not his handmaid. She speaks God's will to the servants at the marriage feast. And she tells the servants to do what Jesus tells them. She speaks for God the Father to Jesus who then has the servants fill six large stone jars with water which he changed into wine fit for a feast. And thus he begins to transform ordinary life into something extraordinary, and he did so to spare his mother and the bridegroom shame.

He was obedient to the human situation, to his humanity, and in that obedience of the Son of God the human was transformed. It was as striking as the transfiguration on Mount Tabor; for if those at the wedding feast could see what Mary heard and saw, it would be as full of power and glory as when Jesus was himself transformed before Peter, James, and John, and they heard the voice from the enveloping cloud say, "This is my Son, the Beloved; with him I am well pleased; listen to him!" (Matthew 17:5–7).

John will write of this first sign of Jesus so that the faithful might know that as the Father spoke of his Beloved Son, saying, "Listen to him," so Mary spoke for her beloved son Jesus, inaugurating his signs on earth with the words, "Do whatever he tells you." And Jesus, at Mary's word that she heard from the Father, told them what to do, namely, listen to her son. That is the kind of force she is in the room, even now as she moves slowly into her final days. The quiet presence, the ongoing force toward the building of the kingdom, the voice that Jesus listens to.

God's Breath

She has loved their home in Ephesus. It is a refuge and a church where the believers gather often to pray and break bread and listen to John teach and preach the resurrection of Jesus. The faithful gather in their own houses, too, for the ceremony of prayer and sharing stories and the breaking of the bread; and she and John go together or separately to the different homes of gathering in order to help and encourage the building up of the kingdom of God.

But there is something special about this home. It is as if the stones of the walls have stored up light within them. And both she and John feel the embrace of the light-filled blocks of stone as soon as they enter. But there is not only the light of the house itself with its warm glow of light; there is also the light of the home they became to each other when Jesus gave them one to the other, mother to son, and son to mother.

No matter how loud the singing of the disciples, or the speaking in tongues, and other manifestations of God's Spirit, when all have returned to their homes again, nothing seems to have disturbed the peace and tranquility of this space they share together, its warmth and light. It feels like a shelter after the storm when the rain begins to patter softly on the roof and you open the shutters to a gentle breeze and the remaining drizzle of rain shimmers in the light of the leaves of the olive trees.

There is always the cleaning up after the meal the disciples share, just as they share their own possessions with the others, but that, too, because the meals are spare and simple, is not so much a cleaning and washing up, as a re-ordering of the space. That ordering then ends up being a re-ordering of the space inside and between her and John so that the rhythm of their relating might once again reflect the quiet movement of the air they breathe.

That is the peace they breathe in the home they have made. But of late she has begun to feel a larger home enveloping her. It opens beyond the door of the house where she and John have lived these many years since, at the behest of Jesus, John took her into his own house. This other home seems to grow beyond the horizons of the four directions of the earth, and beyond the earth, as well. And her own spirit seems to grow, as well, moving in this larger home that must be the eternity Jesus promised his followers, the eternity of the prophets, the eternity John has been talking about recently, the eternity that is a new heaven and a new earth.

John said it would be like the holy city Jerusalem coming down out of heaven from God. And it will be full of peace and its light will be the glory of God. She feels somehow that she is moving already in this new Jerusalem, this mystical city, and it is her home. And she feels its peace, especially when she lies down at night and surrenders her spirit to the mystery who is God.

That is the peace she feels now, even as she is thinking of how wonderful it is that she and John have made this house a home. It is like the whole house is now inside this new city, Jerusalem. She is filled with joy as she lies down more tired than usual.

She closes her eyes, and she is inside the new Jerusalem, it seems, that is beyond her home here in Ephesus. She is in a large field that is inside the new Jerusalem, and she is lying down as in a field of golden ripened wheat. She tries to keep her eyes closed, but the light of the field floods the room where she was trying to sleep, and she is wide awake. She begins to rise. Or are her eyes still closed and she is but dreaming that his hand is reaching down to her? She is still in the beautiful field, but she can hear John turning in his sleep in the other room, though the sound grows fainter and the light grows brighter around her. The over-shadowing cloud is lifting as is she. She sees John. He is sitting up in bed, eyes toward heaven, looking at her. He is smiling. He is lifting his arms as if lifting her, then releasing her like a feather caught on the breath that is the Holy Spirit. Amen. So be it.

Poems

Mary, mother, be my fine
filling, your life shaping mine
I am embryo of me
newly emerging baby

Your life in me is Christ's life
before the growing child's strife

You make me Christ's new body
His Spirit I now embody

through your body's milk and blood
that my inmost being flood

Then am I born, your newborn child
Christ's new face innocent, mild

light shining in the dark inn
your new Bethlehem to begin

MADONNA PIETÁ

Who are you, Mary,
child and broken man
upon your knee?
Both baby and man agree
that you are all-woman,
life-giver, lady of
visions and decisions.

Youth pines that you are
purity unreachable,
and age proclaims you
fertility-fulfilled,
one perfect act
of will—surrender to
Divine Motherhood—
childing you
forever with God.

Filling your womb is he,
the first-born of many
to share divinity
in being reborn through you
and humanity by
lying heavy, broken
in your open lap.

Winter

Mary of Nazareth,
like snow falling
swiftly,
secretly
upon the passive earth,
you cover us
with white warmth,
burrowing under your drifts,
bear-like
in our hibernation
from the heart's stormy season.

DREAM WOMAN

Lady of my woods
the path to you
cuts across
all my desires
and enters the sanctuary
of secluded oaks
swiftly
beneath my feet

I look
for your reflection
in the little stream
that runs beneath
the bridge we built
to watch your image by

And always just
below the silver surface
of this trysting creek
shining coyly
back at me
are you
Mary
Virgin Lady
of my woods

But turning around
to surprise you
at my shoulder

I see only
a face of moon

Again in stillness
you have eluded me
as you slip away
racing deeper
inside my woods

CAROL IN A CLIMATE OF WAR

What music now
twenty-one centuries after
Mary sang in our flesh,

"I am Your servant;
be fashioned in me."
Her words now vie

with words not hers
who opened her womb
to the Angel's word.

Frenetic flapping sings
of fabricated wings
trapped in human words

that refuse the invitation
to embody God's Word.
The powerful screech,

"Glory to us on high,
woe to those who won't
join us in war's chorus."

But Angels sing the antiphon,
"Kneel before the little Word
who's swaddled—wordless."

Baby purls, animal sounds.
Silent Mary, Joseph nearby,
turn our war-cry to lullaby.

GABRIEL

She reminded him of God.
Was it the light of her face
the light in her eyes? Or was
it surprise at his own light
shining when he looked at her?

He longed to walk into her
through her to the other side
as into a bright sunset
and beyond into her heart

and he but a messenger
of the child who'd enter her

ROSARY

Then the train speeds up and slows
before its even rhythm

If you came from heaven to
teach me of your son today

would you come quickly, then
slow down before disappearing

into my daily rosary –
a train of measured beads

beats of metronomic speed
that hold your image longer

like a train even on rails
that define the horizon

of its passing day and night
through my fingers trying to

hold on to what's already
there inside this ancient prayer

MARY IN THE BOUGAINVILLEA

Like a lush rug petals lie
beneath your icon, Mary
Mother of the Cosmic Christ

Flower petals and cosmos
are what you embody here
where human prayer gathers
earth and skies invisible

A rosary of petals
floats in ambiguous air
that strong winds erase, leaving
the bougainvillea, your
image, and heaven and earth

DORMITION OF THE VIRGIN MARY

Flesh of her flesh, flesh of His
She lies there bereft of breath
And speech in arrested time
She rises fleshed and timeless
Breathing Him who breathed her

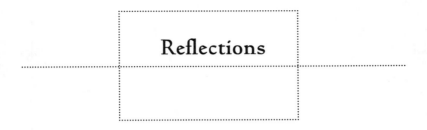

Reflections

While her servant Francis was living in the church of the Virgin Mother of God, he prayed to her who had conceived the Word full of grace and truth, imploring her with continuous sighs to become his advocate. Through the merits of the Mother of Mercy, he conceived and brought to birth the spirit of the truth of the Gospel.

— St. Bonaventure[1]

Losing and Finding Mary

Even after I could no longer feel her presence, she was always there alive on the border between my youth and the new confusing experience in which I could feel nothing. For years she lived on the periphery of my vision, as if I were on a slow train passing a mountain or mesa I had loved and used to climb as a boy. I knew her name, Mary, but I felt no connection except to the train that kept going nowhere, as in a dream of being trapped in a train car whose doors wouldn't open, no matter how many stations we stopped at along the way. The Virgin Mary was always just beyond my emotional reach. And so I lived for years with my most constant feeling being that of abandonment, both by God and by God's Mother Mary.

And so it remained until I fell in love with a real woman who somehow entered my train car and sat down beside me. She was Mary of Nazareth, the Mother of Jesus, and I saw her as a lovely woman, and not as an unattainable woman clothed with the sun and sitting at the left hand of her Son sitting at the right hand of the Father. She was the woman before all the fuss, full of grace of every kind. She was someone fully human, but still someone who seemed remote from me, too good for me to relate to, except as a child might relate to his or her mother. But from then on I began to see Mary as the women in my own life who taught me how to relate to a woman, how to love what before I thought I couldn't love. I learned, in short, what love is and where it leads us.

And then, almost by accident or another circumstance, in my eightieth year I went to Loreto in Italy to visit a family there and if there was time for it, to visit the house of Mary of Nazareth, expecting nothing more than a visit to a shrine of a woman who'd come back into my life. Instead, I had an extraordinary experience such as I'd had only two times before: once at the spot where Thomas à Becket was martyred in Canterbury Cathedral and the other standing in Notre Dame Cathedral looking at the Rose window. The experience was even more striking at Loreto. It was simply that I couldn't leave. I felt almost glued to one of the walls of the shrine that Church tradition believes contains three walls of Mary's house in Nazareth.

I was there with a friend, the writer and pilgrim guide, Bret Thoman, who lives in Loreto with his wife and children. I was aware he was waiting for me outside in the Basilica itself, but something kept holding me there in Mary's house, almost as in an embrace that wanted to leave a lasting memory of love and care. I am not sure how long it was, but when I was finally released and came out into the Basilica, Bret only smiled and said, "You had an experience, didn't you?" And, of course, I had: The Mary of my childhood and the Mary I'd learned to see more as a woman than an icon had welcomed me into her home, and it was good.

These two experiences—meeting the Blessed Virgin Mary again as a real woman and then being invited to her home in Nazareth—come at the end of a long journey in my relationship to the Blessed Virgin Mary and her place in my life and in the life of the Church. And it all began the night I was born.

June 10, 1937. I am born by Caesarian section in St. Mary's Hospital, Gallup, New Mexico. A Franciscan Sister takes me in her arms to the altar of the Blessed Virgin Mary and dedicates me to Mary, patroness of the hospital, and from this moment on, unknown to me, my spiritual mother. And now, having finished these two sentences, a gentle rain falls on my writing hermitage, as if punctuating the event whose implications I would not fully realize until sixteen years later at St. Francis High School Seminary where I was preparing to become a Franciscan Friar and Catholic priest. I prayed at Mary's altar in the seminary chapel every day and in May of my junior year I wrote my first published poem. It appeared in our school magazine, *The Brown and White*, in May, 1954.

A MOMENT WITH MARY
'Tis eventide. The smoke of incense
  And of tapers fades away.
Evening prayers are over. Lies
  Behind us one more day.

One by one we students file
  From our places to her shrine.
Come, 'tis time to pay a visit
  To God's mother and to thine.

Prayerful lips are slowly moving
  Thanking Mary for her care.
Can one read what each is saying
  To his mother, queen so fair?

One more day has faded, Mother,
  In the background of the years.
Make each new day full of goodness
  In our lonesome vale of tears.

Mother dear, time is flying
  And I now must soon depart
'Till tomorrow then, Madonna,
  Hold me near thy loving heart.

It's a sweet, sentimental nineteenth-century poem. And in reading it now, I wonder how my classmates bore the rush of adolescent piety in the lines. But it is indicative of where I was spiritually at that time of my life

But it was the second poem I published in the November issue of *The Brown and White* of the same year, 1954, the beginning of my senior year, that pleases me more, as it did then. I still remember how proud I was that I had written a whole poem that was a metaphor.

MARY
A lovely lily of David's field
  Did God decree
That of a tainted nature
  Would be free.

He breathed into its
Snowy cup of white,
  The breath of life
With abounding grace bedight.

He took this chalice pure
  And on us poured,
His son, our Saviour,
Christ the Lord.

I smile now at the antique sound of the poem and the archaic word, *bedight*, which these many years and poems later I had to look up in my faithful Merriam-Webster's Collegiate Dictionary. It means "array" or "equip," which I didn't use because those terms wouldn't rhyme with "white." At this distance I do admire the young seminarian's ingenuity and perseverance in finding the archaic *bedight*. And to use the English spelling, "Saviour," to have the same assonance look as the word, "poured," in the line above. I had no idea I had that kind of feel for the sound and look of words when I was a teenager.

At the time of both poems' writing, I was deeply immersed in reading and trying to practice *True Devotion to Mary* as defined by St. Louis de Montfort in a book of the same name. Not surprisingly, for a Catholic seminarian in the 1950s, Mary was hugely important. She, God's mother, was a virgin who would help us be "pure," a goal that could have unhealthy consequences for a naïve adolescent boy living in a sheltered high school seminary.

The overemphasis on the soul was for me, and I believe, for other overly serious and scrupulous seminarians, as well, the beginning of a subtle denial of our sexuality and the beginning of a gradual split between body and soul, an ongoing perversion of a healthy, holistic attitude toward oneself and others.

In the desperate attempt to become pure soul and forget the body, an adolescent, especially, could in that milieu become obsessed with the body, the overpowering counter valence to the attempt to separate what God has created as a unified human being, the miracle of body and soul as one person.

In looking back on all of this struggle and turmoil, I now realize that it was mainly myself who was the problem. I was an overly serious and devout teenager and not the "normal" boy slowly becoming a man. And by clinging to a warped idea of Mary, formed largely by pious, warped authors of some of the "spiritual books" in our seminary library, I was really undoing (almost violently) what Mary was about and who she was. It is no wonder that I went through eight years of a dark night of the soul that followed upon my graduation from the high school seminary. It began the very day I put on the Franciscan habit, August 15, 1955, the Feast of the Assumption of the Blessed Virgin Mary into heaven. (I somehow missed the part where she took her body with her.)

Mary certainly was assumed into heaven, I believed, but suddenly I felt nothing for her, I who had gushed over her all through my high school years. She disappeared, and I was left alone, divided by a false spirituality that would in the end be righted by my own Franciscan vocation, my own Franciscan spiritual directors, and the theology of St. Francis that was given its most lucid and profound articulation by another medieval Franciscan Friar, Blessed John Duns Scotus, who was born in 1266, forty years after the death of St. Francis in 1226.

I believed, because I was taught to believe by some over-enthusiastic Jansenistic writers, that the body was evil, the source of sin that Christ came to deliver us from. Christ came to save our souls from the lusts and other evils of the body that imprisons our beautiful souls. Christ is the one who would free the soul from its slavery to the body. But then Blessed John Duns Scotus comes into my life years later, and my whole viewpoint and attitude toward God and the world begins to change.

John Duns Scotus was a medieval Franciscan philosopher/theologian, and his influence on me began already in my final year of undergraduate studies at our Franciscan College in Southfield, Michigan, aptly named Duns Scotus College. I was twenty-two years old and had just made my Solemn Profession of Vows as a Franciscan Friar the year before. The philosophy course I was taking at the time was on the metaphysics of John Duns Scotus, and our teacher was Fr. Roy Effler, OFM, a disciple and student of Fr. Alan Wolter, OFM, whose textbook we were using. I understood relatively little of metaphysics as an academic discipline at the time and was especially nonplussed over Duns Scotus's proof for the existence of God. I was impressed, though, that Fr. Roy needed all the blackboard space on three walls of the classroom to map out what to me seemed an unintelligible proof that took more faith than God's existence did.

But something of that course did register with me. It was an attitude toward reality that was in practice a point of view, a way of seeing, that began with a central teaching of Duns Scotus: The Absolute Predestination and Universal Primacy of Christ.

The first time I uttered that phrase, it was a mouthful, and it still is, but for me the unraveling of what the phrase means changed my whole way of being in the world. The gist of Scotus's take on the Incarnation is that he rejects the view of St. Augustine, St. Thomas Aquinas, and others that the Incarnation is contingent on, that it depends upon, the sin of Adam. In other words, the belief that Christ came primarily to save us from our sins. In the words of St. Augustine, "*O Felix Culpa,*" "O happy fault" that merited such a Savior. The fault, of course is the sin of Adam.

For Scotus it is inconceivable that the miracle of the Incarnation, i.e., God taking on a created nature in Christ, should be conditioned by something so negative as sin. He writes: "I say then that the Fall was not the reason for Christ's predestination. Even if no angel had fallen, nor any human, Christ would still have been predestined—yes, even if no others were to have been created save only Christ."[2]

These words of Scotus establish Christ as the pinnacle of creation, containing in himself the patterns of everything that is created and as the primary intention of God in communicating God's perfections.

The nineteenth-century Jesuit poet, Gerard Manley Hopkins, who was deeply influenced by Duns Scotus, states in one of his sermons, "The first intention of God outside himself, or as they say, *ad extra*, outwards, the first outstress of God's power, was Christ."[3] Simply put, this means that Christ is willed by the Trinity from all eternity, independent of human sin and redemption.

So, for Scotus the Incarnation is an act of love that would have taken place in one form or another whether or not there had been any sin. Hopkins understood this and taught that God as God could not perform the act of an inferior nature; so from all eternity God willed to become a human creature in order to express that aspect of God's love which was impossible for God alone, namely to be loved by someone who was both God and human; in Jesus Christ God could love Himself from within God's creation as a human being.

For Scotus this means that Christ is first in God's intentions. It is Jesus Christ, and Jesus Christ alone, who is infinitely able to render to God supreme glory and perfect love from within created beings as one of them. Another way of saying this is that Christ is the first conceived in the mind of the Creator in projecting a creative plan. That is what is meant by the Absolute Predestination and

Universal Primacy of Christ. Christ is willed freely and lovingly in God, not as an improvisation or second-guess merely to repair a sinful breach. As St. Paul puts it in Colossians:

> [Christ] is the image of the invisible God, the firstborn of all creation; for in him all things in heaven and on earth were created, things visible and invisible, whether thrones or dominions or rulers or powers—all things have been created through him and for him. He himself is before all things, and in him all things hold together. He is the head of the body, the church; he is the beginning, the firstborn from the dead so that he might come to have first place in everything. For in him all the fullness of God was pleased to dwell, and through him God was pleased to reconcile to himself all things, whether on earth or in heaven, by making peace through the blood of his cross. (1:15–20)

It was because Christ was the perfect adorer of God, the perfect bridge between creatures and the Creator, that he could bridge the gap created by sin. Sin was not first in God's intentions; but because we sinned, when God does come among us as Jesus Christ, his perfect adoration ends up being his perfect sacrifice. He didn't come to repair sin, he came to be the firstborn perfect creature; but because we sinned, he showed us just how great is God's love: God not only becomes one of us, but he dies with and for us and made peace "through the blood of his cross."

How, then, does Scotus relate all of the foregoing to Mary?

Duns Scotus was the great champion of the Immaculate Conception of Mary, namely, that she was conceived in her mother's womb without Original Sin. Scotus, of course, was a medieval man; and it wasn't until the late nineteenth century that Mary herself declares to St. Bernadette at Lourdes that her name is "The Immaculate Conception." And it is not until 1854 that Mary's Immaculate Conception becomes a dogma of the Church. Pope Pius IX defined the dogma in his historic Bull, *"Ineffabilis Deus,"* "Ineffable God." In this decree the Pope said explicitly that Mary was predestined "in one and the same decree" with her Son. She shares, as much as a pure creature can, in the primacy and prior predestination of her Son. God decreed Mary, as did her Son, in God's first intentions for creation, unconditioned by sin.

Because of this creative intent on God's part to unite her with Christ as the center of the universe, Mary belongs to the hypostatic order, not in the sense that like Christ she had both a human and divine nature, nor that she was in any way divine, but that she is related to Christ in such a way as to place her in a position far transcending other creatures. From this priority of Mary's predestination flows her Immaculate Conception, her complete preservation from sin, her co-redemptive role in creation, her title as Queen of the Universe, her bodily assumption into heaven, her office as Mediatrix of All Graces. In short, whatever God willed for his Son, he also willed for Mary as much as a creature could receive. As the Scotist scholar and Franciscan friar Alan Wolter puts it:

> Mary is the first creature predestined in Christ. Her relation to Christ is analogous to Christ's relation to God; for just as Christ is the first overflow of God's love for Himself, so Mary is the first outpouring of God's love for Christ. And again, just as God gave Himself to a created nature in the highest possible degree, when the Verbum united Himself hypostatically to that nature, so Christ, the Verbum Incarnatum, gives Himself to a mere

creature in the highest possible way when He becomes her son. And no mere creature ever gave so much to Christ as she who gave Him flesh and blood. As in the natural, so also in the super-natural order. No greater grace ever flowed from love than hers. Here again we have a closed circle, a second creation, complete in the sense that it gives the highest extrinsic glory to Christ.[4]

And here, too, we are closing the circle of this reflection from the sweet, sentimental Mary I knew as a child to Mary, "Virgin Made Church." It is that simple epithet of St. Francis that has made all the difference in my finding Mary again.

"Virgin Made Church." The Second Vatican opens that phrase up in these words:

> In the mystery of the Church which is itself rightly called mother and virgin, the Blessed Virgin stands out in eminent and singular fashion as exemplar of both virgin and mother. Through her faith and obedience she gave birth on earth to the very Son of the Father.... The Son she brought forth is he whom God placed as the first born among many brothers and sisters (Rom 8:29), that is, the faithful, in whose generation and forma-tion she cooperates with a mother's love. (*Lumen Gentium*, 8:63)

So, Mary's virginity is not some kind of strained enclosure or an unnatural denial of the body. It is a choice that leads to a new kind of fruitfulness born of love that is human and inclusive and deeply spiritual, as well. What Mary's choice meant for Mary herself Blessed John Duns Scotus has defined and explained. What fruitfulness means in human lives St. Francis has described in the Second Version of his "Letter to All the Faithful." He writes,

We are mothers of our Lord Jesus Christ when we carry him in our hearts and in our bodies, lovingly and with a pure and sincere conscience, and give birth to him through the working of his grace in us which should shine forth as an example to others. We are his spouses when we are wed to Jesus Christ by the Holy Spirit. We are his brothers and sisters when we do the will of his Father who is in heaven.[5]

One need not be a virgin, of course, to be mother and spouse of Jesus Christ, but voluntary virginity is one way to participate in that kind of fruitfulness. It does not constrain the heart. It liberates it. How that is for Mary is an ever-opening mystery. How it is for others who choose virginity also partakes of mystery and can only be understood in the context of love and what love will do and choose that may seem unnatural or foolish to those who choose another way of being fruitful in Christ. Either way, our choices are only as fruitful as they are rooted in love. What that means and how it plays out is as personal as the way we love and make love-choices on our journey through life.

A Cloud of Unknowing

In the First Book of Kings the priests bring the ark of the covenant to its place in the temple of Solomon "in the inner sanctuary of the house, in the most holy place, underneath the wings of the Cherubim" (1 Kings 8:6). And when the priests leave, "a cloud filled the house of the Lord, so that the priests could not stand to minister because of the cloud" (1 Kings 8:10–11). Then Solomon says, "The Lord has said that he would dwell in thick darkness" (1 Kings 8:12).

And so it is with Mary. A cloud fills and surrounds her, distancing her from our vision so that she, too, seems to dwell in a sort of thick darkness. We know that God dwelt in her more intimately than in any other creature. She did not hold the stone tablets of the law, as the ark of the covenant did, but she held the Word of the living God becoming human in her womb. This is the most significant event in the history of the world, the Incarnation of God; but how it all came to be is surrounded by a cloud, a cloud that an anonymous medieval mystic called "a cloud of unknowing."

What we know of Mary derives from a few sparse references to her in the New Testament, from the testimony of Tradition in the history of the Catholic Church, from the doctrines and dogmas of the Church, and from the mystical apparitions of Mary over the centuries.

As I write these lines, the ink filling an 8 ½ x 11 yellow pad, it is the Feast of Our Lady of Lourdes who identified herself to the young girl, Bernadette Soubirous, as "the Immaculate Conception." Mary identifies herself as one who was free of original sin from the moment she was conceived in the womb of her mother.

Mary is the only human untainted by the consequence of the sin of Adam and Eve, the sin of disobedience to the will of the Creator God. In contrast to Adam and Eve, Mary's was a life of loving obedience to God's Word. That is the belief of the Church. But the particulars of what that meant in Mary's life of mothering Jesus remains in the cloud, except that from time to time there are apparitions of Mary that confirm doctrines and even dogmas that have been believed by the faithful for a long time.

The Catholic dogma of the Immaculate Conception is a good example. In the nineteenth century when Mary revealed herself to Bernadette Soubirous, a young French girl who was gathering wood in a forest, the beautiful woman said that her name is "the Immaculate Conception," a truth that was widely believed for centuries and that was confirmed and made an infallible dogma by Pope Pius IX in 1854.

The revelations of the Blessed Virgin Mary to Bernadette were in 1858, thus confirming in a private apparition what the Pope had proclaimed to the entire Church four years earlier. And from the time of St. Bernadette's visions to the present, Mary has confirmed the authenticity of Bernadette's visions by a plethora of miraculous healings that continue at the Shrine of Our Lady of Lourdes.

The evidence of signs and wonders has been central to the Christian kerygma from the very beginnings of Christianity, the first miracle worker and healer being Jesus himself during the three years of his public life. And Mary's intercession with Jesus goes back to the beginning of Jesus's ministry. Jesus and his mother are at a marriage feast in Cana. The wine has run out and Jesus is informed about what has happened. Jesus is reluctant to do anything about it because, he says, his time has not yet come. But Mary intercedes and tells the stewards to do what Jesus tells them to do. It is as if she didn't hear him or is telling him that yes, it is time. And Jesus accedes and changes his mind and changes water into wine to save the young married couple embarrassment.

This is such a human, endearing vignette. But it is also, as John the Evangelist says, the first of Jesus's signs. It is through the intercession of Mary, his mother, that Jesus works the first public sign of his divinity. He "revealed his glory, and his disciples believed in him" (John 2:11).

Then John says, "After this he went down to Capernaum with his mother, his brothers, and his disciples; and they remained there a few days" (John 2:12). Does Mary just go down with Jesus, his brothers, and his disciples, or is Mary one of his disciples from the beginning of his first sign? How much is she with him once his public ministry begins? One thing is certain. She is intimately involved with the revelation of Jesus's divine ministry through signs and wonders. She intercedes with him as only a mother could, so that, from the very beginning Mary is there, not only in his life upon earth, but in his ministry, as well. But that is so small an opening into the mystery of the Blessed Virgin Mary.

What we don't know is how much Mary was present as Jesus went about preaching and teaching and healing. That is a part of our cloud of unknowing about Mary, but what we do know is a lot, considering how little we know of Mary from Scripture itself.

We know a lot because Mary is writ large in the Tradition of the Church and in the testimony of the Fathers of the Church and in the proclamations of the ongoing doctrines by the Holy See. And she continues to reveal new aspects of who she is in private revelations to individual Christians throughout the centuries. The cloud is beginning to be less dense, less impenetrable, and a whole theology of Mary continues to grow and enlighten her role in the history of salvation. But as with God and with Jesus, the Christ, there remains a cloud of unknowing around Mary. It clouds the impenetrable sanctuary of the mystery of who she is in God that is never wholly transparent, but continues to draw us in as far as our human minds and hearts can go.

Mother of God

Of all the titles and epithets of Mary, the ones that make her most human and real to us are those relating to her motherhood.

Mary, Mother of Jesus. She is not a goddess. She is a woman who became a mother, and not just *a* mother, but *the* mother. This motherhood was central to St. Francis of Assisi's devotion to Mary. His first biographer, Blessed Thomas of Celano, wrote, "Toward the Mother of Jesus he was filled with an inexpressible love, because it was she who made the Lord of Majesty our brother."[6] And St. Francis himself writes in his Letter to the Whole World, "How right it is that we honor so highly the Virgin Mary, for she carried Jesus in her most holy womb."[7]

There is something about a nourishing love that was central to the spirituality of St. Francis. He used to say to his Brothers that they were to love one another, as far as grace enables them to do so, the way a mother loves and nourishes the child of her flesh. And for St. Francis Mary was *the* mother because of the way she loved and nourished Jesus (cf. St. Francis, Rule of 1221, Chapter IX).

In the overall narrative arc of Jesus's life on earth Mary is for the most part the one in the background, the silent, unobserved other who is taken for granted by the narrators of the Gospels and the writers of the canonical letters. When she does move to the forefront, as at the Marriage Feast of Cana where she takes charge of the situation and is the catalyst for his first public miracle,

Mary emerges as decisive and confident. And when she hears of her cousin Elizabeth's pregnancy, she goes immediately into the hill country to be there for her cousin. She is also the one who confronts her young son Jesus when he stays behind in Jerusalem without telling his parents.

But for most of the public life of Jesus Mary is silent. She is silent when she meets him on the way to Calvary, she is silent beneath the cross, and she is silent when Jesus rises from the dead and subsequently ascends into heaven. And she is silent when her Spouse, the Holy Spirit, descends upon her and the apostles in the upper room after the ascension of Jesus.

Is this simply because the Gospel writers were men and didn't notice her, or was this God's intent from all eternity: namely, that the most important formator of the personality of the human Jesus, his mother Mary, would remain largely hidden until that time when she would be revealed through visions given us through the centuries, visions given to children and those on the margins of self-important societies?

Ironically, she who was one of the most silent and hidden persons during Jesus's lifetime, is now in recent history the most verbal and revealed of salvation history personages. She appears in Mexico to the peasant Juan Diego walking along a road; in France to the girl Bernadette of Lourdes when she is gathering firewood in the forest; in Fatima, Portugal, to three children on their way home from tending a flock of sheep; and in Medjugorje in the area of Bosnia-Herzegovina, Mary appeared to six local children, the visions beginning in 1981. In all these apparitions she is not a silent, retiring woman; she appears as the apocalyptic woman of St. John the Evangelist's book of *Revelation*. She is the woman clothed with the sun whose child slays the satanic snake. Her messages are detailed and relate to the whole world, to the planet and its future, to the redemptive power of love to transform the increasingly deteriorating planet.

To very briefly summarize the messages of Mary to the world: At Lourdes she reminds us that God is love and loves us as we are. Mary asks St. Bernadette to open her heart to Mary's message of love. At Guadalupe Mary asks the Aztec convert, Juan Diego, to have a church built in her honor and then miraculously imprints her image on his cloak, the image of the woman of the Apocalypse as an olive-skinned woman, pregnant with Jesus. She is clothed in a turquoise mantle and is surrounded by rays of light. At Guadalupe Mary has become the symbol of the dignity of indigenous peoples and those living on the margins of society. At Medjugorje Mary tells the young visionaries that we are to pray often, to fast, and to do penance. At Fatima Mary offers a Peace Plan from Heaven: We are to amend our lives, or we will continue to endure wars and other sufferings. We are to pray the Rosary every day for the peace of the world and the end of war. It seems that in relatively recent times Mary is the preferred messenger of the Trinity. She is indeed Our Lady of the Angels, God's messengers. She is in recent times *the* Messenger of God.

Christ and His Mother

How to further explain the tremendous emphasis on the role of the Virgin Mary within Catholicism? Usually in dire circumstances or need the first prayer that comes to a Catholic's lips is the "Hail Mary." And how to explain the seemingly countless shrines and churches dedicated to Mary?

There are many explanations, from piety to custom to Church teaching to history to the need for a feminine dimension to religion. But fundamentally, the answer to Mary's role and popularity among believers is Christ himself. It is only in the mystery of Christ that the mystery of Mary is made clear.

Just as she gives birth to Christ who is the head of the Mystical Body, so she gives birth to the Church itself, which is the Mystical Body of Christ.

Christ came among us as God and man by means of a human birth through Mary, the Spouse of the Holy Spirit. In turn, we are born into new life in Christ through Mary who is Mother of the Church. In addition, Mary is also *the* image of what the Church herself is, namely, a new community whose bond is faith in Jesus Christ, Son of God, born of the Virgin Mary. We, then, as brothers and sisters of Christ, have Mary as our spiritual mother. We are spiritually reborn through the motherhood of Mary.

Jesus says to us from the cross in the person of John the Evangelist, "Behold your mother." And to his mother he says, "Behold your son" (or daughter, as the case may be). To believe that the spiritual motherhood of Mary is true for all of us takes the same kind of faith that Mary herself had when she said, "Behold the handmaid of the Lord. May it be done to me according to your word." That is the faith that is necessary for the new reality that is the Mystical Body of Christ. It is a faith in the word of God as it is received and acted upon in the Church. "Be it done unto us according to your word, Lord, as it was done in your and our mother Mary.

Our Mother Mary. She is the image of the Church: virginal, yet always giving birth to Christ in those who believe, as she believed that God's Word became flesh in Jesus, and in us who believe, and who, like Mary, believe that Jesus is the Word made flesh. The Incarnation happened through Mary's faith that the word spoken to her by the Angel Gabriel was God's Word. And it was Mary's yes to that word that effected the enfleshment of the Word as the living flesh and blood of Jesus Christ who is both Eternal Word and the human being, Jesus, the Son of Mary.

This is the theology, the teaching of the Church, that is behind the role and popularity of the Virgin Mary in salvation history. It is the reason we pray over and over again in the rosary, "Hail Mary, full of grace, the Lord is with you. Blessed are you among women, and blessed is the fruit of your womb, Jesus. Holy Mary, Mother of God, pray for us sinners now and at the hour of our death. Amen."

The Mother of Jesus of Nazareth

Since Jesus was both God and a man, he had his mother's genes and was deeply influenced genetically, as most humans are, by his mother. He was Mary's son, prompting us to imagine how Mary herself was in fact revealed in the person of her son.

She would also have been the first person to tell her son stories, stories that could have been the source of some of the parables Jesus told, like the poor widow or the kingdom of heaven being like rising, yeasted, dough. Did she tell him stories of his birth in Bethlehem, of the strange visitors from the East who brought him gold, frankincense, and myrrh? Or of the shepherds to whom an angel announced good tidings? Or the prophecy of Simeon and the prophetess Anna when Joseph and Mary presented the baby Jesus in the temple? Or of Joseph's dreams and the flight into Egypt to escape King Herod's slaughter of innocent male babies? Or of the people they met in the Jewish community in Egypt? Did she sing lullabies to Jesus, and what games did they play together? And what ways of doing things did he learn from his mother? And how did they pray together?

And what did Jesus see his mother doing? Did she, like the typical Jewish mother, spend time mending, her workbasket by her side? And did she, from time to time, sit spinning? Certainly, she would have spent time preparing meals of barley bread, of lentils with oil or honey. She would have cooked beans and fixed meals of tomatoes or asparagus and enjoyed large radishes soaked in wine. Onions, too, would have been plentiful, and lots of fruit like pears and peaches, dates and plums and figs, melons and pomegranates. The family would have eaten fish and, probably only rarely, meat such as lamb or goat.

All of which is to say that Jesus was not born and raised in a bubble. He had a mother who showed him manners and proper eating habits and how to act and interact with others. None of these questions and imaginings are addressed in the Gospel, except when Mary tells the stewards at the Marriage Feast of Cana to do whatever Jesus tells them to do, and Jesus acquiesces to his mother's wishes. He was obedient to her, as he was disobedient by not telling Mary and Joseph that he was staying behind in the Temple when they went up to Jerusalem together. And when, on that occasion, he was questioned and indirectly reprimanded by Mary, Scripture says that Jesus then "went down with them and came to Nazareth, and was obedient to them. His mother treasured all these things in her heart. And Jesus increased in wisdom and in years, and in divine and human favor" (Luke 2:51–52).

What depths of meditation are here when we open our minds and imaginations to the mystery of the hidden lives of Mary and her son, Jesus, of how they related to one another, and of how they lived together in Nazareth. What spiritual energy is contained and released for us in the images and scenes we create or receive in the silence of prayerful meditation.

Litany

Queen of Angels
You're up early
Washing, baking, sweeping,
Young country girl
From a scorned province
....
Wife of a carpenter
Mother of a convict
Cause of our joy.
> —Anne Porter, *An Altogether Different Language*

The Litany of the Blessed Virgin Mary. How many titles Mary has! The poet Anne Porter extrapolates on two of Mary's titles, "Queen of Angels" and "Cause of Our Joy," in the last stanzas of her poem, "Cause of Our Joy," quoted above. How succinctly Porter has concretized the human, womanly actions that make Mary seem close to us. These eight lines are so real, so perfect an expression of why we love Mary: She is one of us, and yet she is more. She is the whole litany of names and titles she has garnered over the centuries and which became the Litany of Our Lady of Loreto. The original version of the litany we have today was approved by Pope Sixtus V in 1587.

These are the invocations added by future generations: "Queen of All Saints" (Pius VII), "Queen Conceived without Original Sin," (Pius IX), "Queen of the Most Holy Rosary" and "Mother of Good

Counsel" (Leo XIII), "Queen of Peace" (Benedict XV), "Queen
Assumed into Heaven" (Pius XII), "Mother of the Church" and
"Queen of Families" (John Paul II), "Mother of Hope," "Mother
of Mercy," and "Comfort of Migrants" (Pope Francis).

This then is the full Litany of the Blessed Virgin Mary that originated at her shrine in Loreto, Italy:

Lord have mercy.
Christ have mercy.
Lord have mercy.
Christ hear us.
Christ graciously hear us.
God the Father of Heaven,
have mercy on us.
God the Son, Redeemer of the world,
God the Holy Spirit,
Holy Trinity, one God,

Holy Mary,
pray for us,
Holy Mother of God,
Holy Virgin of virgins,
Mother of Christ,
Mother of the Church,
Mother of divine grace,
Mother of hope,
Mother most pure,
Mother most chaste,
Mother inviolate,
Mother undefiled,
Mother most amiable,
Mother most admirable,

Mother of good counsel,
Mother of our Creator,
Mother of our Savior,
Mother of mercy,
Virgin most prudent,
Virgin most venerable,
Virgin most renowned,
Virgin most powerful,
Virgin most merciful,
Virgin most faithful,
Mirror of justice,
Seat of wisdom,
Cause of our joy,
Spiritual vessel,
Vessel of honor,
Singular vessel of devotion,
Mystical rose,
Tower of David,
Tower of ivory,
House of gold,
Ark of the Covenant,
Gate of Heaven,
Morning star,
Health of the sick,
Refuge of sinners,
Comfort of migrants,
Comforter of the afflicted,
Help of Christians,
Queen of Angels,
Queen of Patriarchs,
Queen of Prophets,
Queen of Apostles,

Queen of Martyrs,
Queen of Confessors,
Queen of Virgins,
Queen of all Saints,
Queen conceived without original sin,
Queen assumed into heaven,
Queen of the most holy Rosary,
Queen of families,
Queen of peace.

Lamb of God, who takes away the sins of the world,
spare us, O Lord.
Lamb of God, who takes away the sins of the world,
graciously hear us, O Lord.
Lamb of God, who takes away the sins of the world,
Have mercy on us.

Pray for us, O Holy Mother of God,
That we may be made worthy of the promises of Christ.

Grant, we beseech You, O Lord God, that we your servants may
enjoy perpetual health of mind and body; and by the glorious
intercession of the Blessed Mary, ever Virgin, may be delivered
from present sorrow and obtain eternal joy. Through Christ Our
Lord. Amen.

A Reflection on Lines from "The Blessed Virgin Compared to the Air We Breathe"

This is Gerard Manley Hopkins, that extraordinary English Jesuit wordsmith, comparing Mary to the air we breathe:

> I say that we are wound
> With mercy round and round
> As if with air: the same
> Is Mary, more by name.

For Hopkins we are rounded, surrounded by mercy the way we are with air. And even more so is Mary rounded so, since she is Mary, the Mercy of God. Her very name indicates what it is she surrounds us with, namely, her merciful self. Who, though, is she?

> She, wild web, wondrous robe,
> Mantles the guilty globe.
> Since God has let dispense
> Her prayers his providence.

She is like a web in the wilderness or like a wondrous robe that like a mantle covers the guilty world. She is that mantle because God lets her prayers dispense his providence. But she is more than that, more than someone who dispenses alms to us.

> Nay, more than almoner
> The sweet alms' self is her

And men are meant to share
Her life as life does air.

She herself is the very alms we receive. She is the gift that we are
meant to share the way life itself shares the air.

If I have understood,
She holds high motherhood
Towards all our ghostly good.

The "ghostly good" is our spiritual good and Mary is mother of
the spiritual good that comes to us

And plays in grace her part
About man's beating heart.

Mary's part is to grace our beating heart, but how? By

Laying like air's fine flood,
The deathdance in his blood;
Yet no part but will
Be Christ our Savior still.

Yet what she gives us will be what she gave Christ. For just as she
gave Christ humanity, which will die, she now gives us Divinity,
as it were, his Spirit, making us reborn as new Christs who will
live forever with him.

Of her flesh he took flesh:
He does take fresh and fresh,
Though much the mystery how,
Not flesh but spirit now
And makes, O marvellous
New Nazareths in us.

In the Spirit, through the mystery of Mary's motherhood, he lives in us the way he did in Mary's womb, though now she continues to conceive him again and again, new "Christs" spiritually conceived in her as when she conceived Jesus Christ in Nazareth

> Where she shall yet conceive
> Him, morning, noon, and eve:
> New Bethlems, and he born
> There, evening, noon, and morn—

As she continues to conceive new Christs in new Nazareths, she continues to birth new Christs in new "Bethlems" (Bethlehems) over and over again.

> Bethlem or Nazareth
> Men here may draw like breath
> More Christ and baffle death;
> Who, born so, comes to be
> New self and nobler me
> In each one and each one
> More makes, when all is done,
> Both God's and Mary's Son.

Each one of us in our rebirth in grace becomes more than we would be, were we only flesh and blood, the child of our human mother. But through the grace of Baptism we have a new mother, Mary, the mother of Jesus who is the Christ. We become more. We become brothers and sisters of Christ, sons and daughters, of the Virgin Mary through grace.

Now all of this is said more succinctly by Hopkins, more beautifully. He emphasizes words by putting them in new combinations. For example, instead of saying,

Since God has let her
prayers dispense his providence,

Hopkins says,

Since God has let dispense
Her prayers his providence,

thereby discovering a rhyme in "dispense" and "providence" as a way of enhancing the sound, making the reader see on the page the relationship between dispensing and providence in Mary's life, making the reader/speaker slow down and parse out the meaning. Hopkins's craft makes the two lines more meaningful for the reader who has to work to understand that Hopkins is talking about the mystery of Mary as Mediatrix of God's providential gifts of grace. And the highest of all graces she dispenses is the grace of Mary herself. He writes, as quoted above, of Mary as almoner, but

Nay, more than almoner,
The sweet alms' self is her,

the two lines rhyming again as they do throughout this very long poem that I have quoted sparsely and not in full. They say that Mary is both the almoner and the alms. The reader has to work hard to get to the core of what Hopkins is saying, but once that core is opened up, what riches are revealed, what clarifying arrangements of words toward new understandings! And the reader invariably sees that the unique way Hopkins says things is not for eccentricity's sake but for new meanings revealed in the way it is said.

The poet Alexander Pope once said,

True wit is nature to advantage dressed;
What oft was thought, but ne'er so well express'd.

There is truth in this couplet, but in Hopkins, I often find that the way he expresses things is more than just something we often think but have never seen expressed so well. In Hopkins the way he expresses things is often not just a new way of expressing something, but a new knowing. It is something we have felt perhaps but didn't know we knew until Hopkins expressed it. The way he says things is the knowing. It yields new knowledge not just a new way of saying something we already knew. And that is the genius of Hopkins and the genius of "The Blessed Virgin Compared to the Air We Breathe." There is a whole theology of Mary contained in three or four pages of a text that consists of rhyming couplets.

The text itself is elliptical, meaning that Hopkins leaves things out, omits words that in our working out of the meaning we suddenly "see the words" he leaves out, and in supplying the words left out, we understand how rich is the text that even omitted words begin to appear and enrich the whole experience of the poem itself.

Poetry written about the Blessed Virgin throughout the ages is a rich source of knowledge of Mary and of the devotion and mariology of the times in which the poems were written. And one of the greatest poets to write of Mary in the nineteenth century is the Jesuit poet, Gerard Manley Hopkins who ends "The Blessed Virgin Compared to the Air We Breathe" with a prayer:

Be thou then, O thou dear
Mother, my atmosphere;
My happier world, wherein
To wend and meet no sin;

Above me, round me lie
Fronting my froward eye
With sweet and scarless sky;
Stir in my ears, speak there
Of God's love, O live air,
Of patience, penance, prayer:
World-mothering air, air wild,
Wound with thee, in thee isled,
Fold home, fast fold thy child.

Sermon for a Feast of Mary

Mary is the greatest of all women because she was given the special graces she needed to be the mother of Jesus, the Son of God. And she was, on her own part, the greatest of all mothers because she unselfishly thought of others first. She thought of the needs of others before she thought of her own needs.

For example, when the Angel Gabriel told her that the Holy Spirit would overshadow her and she would be the mother of Jesus, he waited for her consent. And Mary said, "Be it done to me according to God's word." She didn't say, "But what about me? What is going to happen to me? What will others say when they see that I am pregnant? Who will ever believe that I am pregnant, not because I slept with a man, but because the Holy Spirit overshadowed me, and I became pregnant with God's Son?" No, Mary did not think of herself. She thought of God and God's request of her so that God's Word could become human through her. She simply said, "Yes. Be it done unto me according to Your word."

Nor did Mary begin to brood or worry about herself once she had consented to be the mother of Jesus. Rather she immediately made preparations to visit and be with her cousin Elizabeth, who, the Angel had told Mary, was pregnant in her old age. As soon as Mary hears of Elizabeth's need, she goes to Elizabeth to be with her and help her who was pregnant with the man who would become John the Baptist, the one who would prepare the way for her son, Jesus. Mary hears the Angel's news about Elizabeth and, though pregnant herself, she goes to the aid of another pregnant woman, her older cousin, Elizabeth.

And later when Mary and Joseph present the baby Jesus in the temple, she hears from the prophet Simeon that her little baby will grow up to be a sign of contradiction and that a sword will pierce her own heart. Mary doesn't collapse when she hears that a sword will pierce her heart; she worries instead about her baby. What does it mean that he will be a sign of contradiction? What will happen to him? Will he be hurt or die before her? Is that the sword that will pierce her heart, that her son will somehow perish? What can I do to help him, she wonders? Not what is going to happen to me, but what is going to happen to my son?

Mary is the model of what it means to love because love means helping those who need us, even when we ourselves might be in need. Mary is not self-absorbed. She even teaches her son, Jesus, that those in need take precedence even over the ministry or work we think is all important. At the Marriage Feast of Cana, for example, it is Mary who notices that they've run out of wine. And she then tells Jesus. But he says, "What am I supposed to do about it? My hour has not yet come." And Mary, ignoring him, turns to the servants and says, "Do whatever he tells you." She is saying to her son, "This IS your hour. They need you now." And Jesus then works his first miracle; he turns the water into wine. His mother, who always thinks first of others in need, tells Jesus that his hour is when people need him.

What about us? Who do we spend most our time thinking about? Whose needs are always on our mind? Isn't it usually ourselves? But what is Mary telling us? Mary is our spiritual mother, and she is saying to us, as she said to her son, "Don't forget those who have a more pressing need than you do. Remember to remember others. How can you be of help?"

Jesus himself defined his mother as one who lives out the command of charity, the command to love God and our neighbor. Once when his disciples said that his mother and his brothers were outside waiting to see him, Jesus said,

> "Who are my mother and my brothers?" And looking at those who sat around him, he said, "Here are my mother and my brothers! Whoever does the will of God is my brother and sister and mother." (Mark 3:31-35)

What a definition of his mother Mary! She does the will of God. She hears God's word and immediately goes out and does what God's word tells her to do. And that's usually where we tend to fail: We hear God's word in the readings of the Mass, for example, but are slow in acting, slow in trying to do what God tells us is his will.

Let us pray, then, to Mary to help us think of others, first to think of God, who is *the* Other, and then of others who come into our lives or pass our way. There's a lot of love we have for ourselves. We need to think how we can share with others some of the time and preoccupation we spend on ourselves. That is Mary's message for us today: Remember to remember others, especially those in need.

St. Clare of Assisi and Mary

In a book that purports to be a Franciscan book of Mary, it would be a curious omission not to include St. Clare of Assisi. She is the first Franciscan woman and was received into the Order by St. Francis himself in the little chapel of St. Mary of the Angels located on the plain below Assisi. St. Clare brings a strong feminine dimension to the Franciscan charism, but unlike St. Francis, St. Clare has left us no monograph or prayer or salutation to Mary. We, do, however, have from Sister Benvenuta of Assisi in her deposition in the proceedings of "The Process of Canonization," the testimony of a vision that suggests St. Clare must have had a deep devotion to the Blessed Virgin Mary:

> Then that witness [Sr. Benvenuta] began lovingly to think about the manifold and amazing holiness of that Lady Clare. As she was thinking, it seemed to her that the whole heavenly court was on the move and was drawing near to honor this saint. In particular our glorious Madonna, the blessed Virgin Mary, was getting some of her garments ready in order to clothe this new saint....
>
> On the third day before the death of the blessed memory of the Lady and Sister, Saint Clare, [the witness] was weeping at the passing of such and so great a one as their mother, she was sitting beside the bed of that Lady. And, while nobody was speaking to her, that lady [Clare] began to commend her soul, speaking in this way:
>
> > Go in peace, because you will have a good escort, because the One who created you already foresaw that you would be

made holy and then, when he had created you, he breathed into you the Holy Spirit and then he watched you as a mother watches her little son.

This witness, with other thoughts and images, suddenly saw with the eyes of her head, a great multitude of virgins clothed in white. All of them had crowns on their heads. And they came and entered through the door of that room which led to the above mentioned mother Saint Clare. Among those virgins there was one greater and above all the rest—she would not be able to say more than that—but she was beautiful above all the others. And over her crown she had a golden apple like a censor from which there came out so much splendor that it seemed to cast light throughout the whole house.

Those virgins all drew near to the bed of the aforesaid mother Saint Clare, and that Virgin who seemed the greater first covered her in her bed with the finest cloth, so fine that through its great subtlety Madonna Clare, although she was covered with it, even so she was able to see. Then that Virgin of the virgins, the one who was the greater, lowered her face over the face of the aforesaid virgin Saint Clare, or perhaps above her chest—because this witness was not very well able to discern the one from the other. When she had done this, then they all disappeared....

This testimony for the canonization of St. Clare was given at San Damiano Monastery by Sr. Benvenuta, who in the medieval *Legend of St. Clare* maintains she simultaneously had the same vision that Clare was having.

When I began researching, trying to find a writing of Clare that spoke of Mary, I couldn't remember ever reading or hearing of Clare writing anything about Mary. And as I scoured the medieval sources, and began asking others who know such things, there was nothing of substance, at least nothing that has been preserved, except by the grace of God, Sister Benvenuta's testimony on the death of St. Clare. What a find that was!

I had read that testimony many years ago, but had forgotten that it was Mary who came to Clare on her death bed. Perhaps it was my own devotion to St. Clare that kept me looking, but I just knew that Clare had to have had a relationship with Mary who is so prominently painted at the foot of the Cross of San Damiano that Clare meditated upon every day of her life in the monastery of San Damiano. The Cross she called the Mirror. The Cross she asked Agnes to contemplate:

> Gaze into this mirror every day, O Queen, Bride of Jesus Christ, and constantly see your own face reflected in it. …For in that mirror shine blessed poverty, holy humility, love beyond words….
>
> Turn your mind I say, to the border of this mirror; to the poverty of Him who was placed in a manger and wrapped in tiny garments. O wonderful humility! O astounding poverty![8]

We know from this passage that Clare meditated on the birth of Jesus and would have known who it was that placed her baby in a manger and "wrapped him in tiny garments." But in every scene St. Clare writes about, it is always Christ who is the center, Christ who is the Spouse and Lover of the soul. And in her Letters to Agnes, it is Christ whom she writes about, Christ she puts before Agnes as the reason to embrace the poor contemplative life that St. Clare lived with the other Poor Ladies at San Damiano.

So it is interesting that it is not Christ but Mary who accompanies Clare into heaven; it is Mary who will bring Clare to her Lord Jesus Christ who, Clare wrote, is her Spouse, her son, and her brother, indicating that Clare, like Mary, is a virgin who is fruitful, giving birth to Christ, loving him, calling him spouse and son and brother.

This is mystical language, mystical imagery, that reaches its apogee in Clare's Fourth Letter to Agnes of Prague. Agnes, like Clare, was a lady of the nobility, the daughter of the King of Bohemia, and whose hand was sought by the Emperor Frederick II. Clare, too, was of the nobility, the lesser nobility of Assisi. Her mother, Ortolana, was descended from Charlemagne, and her father Favarone was of the noble house of the Offreduccio.

In writing to Agnes, then, who had given up the trappings of royalty, including the right to marry noble, even royal, men, Clare uses the images of a new royalty and a new Spouse, the Lord Jesus Christ. She writes in her Second Letter:

> Embrace the poor Christ, O poor virgin. See Him, made contemptible for you and follow, being made contemptible for Him in the world. Your Bridegroom, who is the most beautiful of the sons of humanity, for your salvation was made the most vile of men, despised, beaten and many times whipped all over His whole body, dying on the cross in the depths of anguish. O most noble queen, gaze, consider, long to imitate. If you suffer with Him, then you will reign with Him; grieving with Him, then you will rejoice with Him; dying with Him on the cross of torments, then you will possess heavenly mansions with Him in the splendour of the saints.[9]

Within such Royal imagery, Mary would be the Queen Mother of Heaven, the way to the King's heart. No wonder, then, that it is Mary who leads Clare into Paradise to the throne of Clare's

Beloved, the Poor King, Jesus Christ, of whom Clare wrote these beautiful words in Letter One:

> Loving Him, You are chaste; touching Him, You are made pure, taking Him to Yourself, You are a virgin. His resources are stronger, His generosity more heavenly, His appearance more beautiful, His love sweeter, and his every grace more attractive.[10]

It is for such a Spouse and such a Lord that Mary covers Clare's bed with "the most delicate cloth so fine," thereby placing Clare among the fruitful virgins of the Mystical Body of Christ. For such Virgins, Mary is the model, the Virgin of virgins, whose way is the way of Mary, who, in the words of St. Francis, is "Virgin made church."

Mary and Us

The distinguished Paraguayan writer, Eduardo Galeano, in one of his short, short stories writes:

> Oriol Vall, who works with newborns at a hospital in Barcelona, says that the first human gesture is the embrace. After coming into the world, at the beginning of their days, babies wave their arms as if seeking someone. Other doctors, who work with people who already lived their lives, say that the aged, at the end of their days, die trying to raise their arms.[11]

The baby's tiny hands and arms wave, trying to find the intimate food of mother's breast. Years later dying hands and arms reach out for the intimate food of embrace. Baby Jesus's tiny arms and hands waving, reaching instinctively for his mother Mary's breast. The dying man Jesus, his hands nailed to the wood of a cross, unable to reach out for his Father in heaven or to his mother standing beneath, his body hanging helpless in agony. Mary in the end holding his lifeless body in her lap, her left hand, in Michelangelo's Pietá, stretched out in humble submission to the Father, "Be it done unto me according to your word," her right hand holding her dead son, her fingers sunk deep in his flesh in a gesture saying "No, not this, not my son." That tragic tension between surrender and disbelief that tries to hold on, mirrors all of us who are born reaching out for the food of intimacy and who die trying to lift our arms to embrace and be embraced by our mother who birthed us and our spiritual mother who rebirthed us into a new life in God. Mother. Food. Intimacy. The images of the Incarnation and the death of Jesus. Mary is there, his mother and ours. She is there in our beginning and in our end. And in her Assumption she, with the Father and the Son, is there in our final embrace of the intimacy we were born for. All of it in the Spirit, which overshadowed her and returned at Pentecost to over-shadow the disciples and us in our Baptism and Confirmation, our new birth and new life of purpose in the Mystical Body of Christ. Mary. She is the one who is there when we are born and when we live and when we die. Mother. Mary. Intimate Presence. Pray for us "now and at the hour of our death."

Afterword

In the 2020 coronavirus pandemic, as in all diseases, we wait. We sit or stand or lie down and wait. We wait when there's nothing more that we can do. We wait impatiently or with panic or anger. We wait and fidget and walk or run.

Or, we do more. We try to turn waiting into something fruitful and good. Just with that change of attitude, something more begins to happen. We begin to learn the richness of waiting, of slowing down, of looking and listening, allowing the world around us and within us to work on us. We begin to understand what it means to receive what is being offered to us every day: the lovescape of God's handiwork within and around us. We begin to see and hear as we did as a child.

This is especially true when we feel helpless to *do* anything to change our circumstances. We begin to just *be*. And at some point from within comes the voice,

> Be still and know that I am God.
> Be still and know that I am.
> Be still and know that I…
> Be still and know that …
> Be still and know…
> Be still and…
> Be still.
> Be.

This is the progression of contemplation, and it takes a lot of time and waiting and contemplating to get to complete surrender to the final injunction, "Be."

Every year for the past ten years or so I have entered into a hermitage for a time, usually three months. I wait and pray and write, trying to enter the silence of my solitude. But it has taken the coronavirus pandemic for me to see how far I still am from simply being. I keep trying to do something, to at least leave the hermitage and travel home to the friary, even when it's still not safe to travel. I keep trying to go home to my friary because "it's time" to do so. But I am forced to wait, to be, instead of to do.

How much is revealed about who we really are when we are forced to wait, especially when we're not sure what we're waiting for. Is that what Mary was doing—just waiting and praying—when the undreamed of annunciation happened: Gabriel invading her private waiting, announcing that the Lord was with her? She was being told that whoever it was she was waiting for was greater than she imagined and was already there: the Word of God.

And Mary says, "Be it done unto me according your word." It's interesting that Mary says, "your word," and not "your will." But, of course, it was the words of God she was hearing in the words of Gabriel. But it was more than those words speaking; it was the Word, the Second Person of the Blessed Trinity. And in Franciscan theology the emphasis on the Word of God in the Incarnation is central, especially in the theology of the great medieval Franciscan theologian, St. Bonaventure.

Ilia Delio, the contemporary Franciscan theologian, writes:

> Bonaventure emphasized that it is the Word who became flesh and not simply "God." Often, we hear the Incarnation described as "God becoming human" but Bonaventure clarifies this by

affirming that it is the *Word* of God that takes on our humanity.... Everything that exists in creation is grounded in the Word of God (and not in the Father or Spirit).... He describes the Incarnation as the work of the Trinity insofar as the entire Trinity is focused in the Word who takes on our humanity.... As eternal Word Christ is the center of the Trinity; as incarnate Word he is center of creation; as inspired Word he is center of the human heart.[12]

And now this Word of God, the second Person and center of the Blessed Trinity was waiting for Mary, for her response to be mother of the Word who wills to be born in and through her. God needed only her consent to let it be, this tremendous miracle of Grace: the enfleshment of God in and through her womb; everything contained within the Word spoken in the depths of the Trinity was now somehow to be placed within her womb.

And to her question of how this was to be, the Angel Gabriel answers that the Holy Spirit would come upon her. And Mary answers, as all her prayer of silence and waiting prepared her for: "Be it done to me according to your word."

So it was for Mary; so it can be for us who wait in silent prayer seemingly unable to do anything to change our circumstances. We can choose to be and let God do. We can choose to let the Holy Spirit work, let the Holy Spirit come upon us that the Word might be born again in and through us. We can be still, and let the Word send down His Spirit.

No angel may appear, no words heard with our ears, but something happens within, an inner hearing of something we know we have to respond to. We hope we can say yes, even when it seems unrealistic or foolish to those who cannot see and cannot hear the Word of God available to those who believe in and love God.

Pope Francis's Prayer to Mary During the Coronavirus

O Mary, Health of the Sick
you always shine on our path
as a sign of salvation and of hope.
We entrust ourselves to you.
You know what we need
and we are sure you will provide,
so that as in Cana of Galilee,
we may return to joy and to feasting
after this time of trial.

Help us, Mother of Divine Love,
to do as we are told by Jesus,
who has taken upon himself our sufferings
and carried our sorrows,
leading us through the cross
to the joy of the resurrection. Amen.

—March 2020 (adapted)

Prayers

The Hail Mary

Hail Mary, full of grace, the Lord is with you.
    Blessed are you among women, and blessed
    is the fruit of your womb, Jesus.

Holy Mary, mother of God, pray for us sinners
    now and at the hour of our death. Amen

*The first part of this prayer is from the infancy narratives of the
Gospel of Luke. The closing petition came into general use during
the fourteenth or fifteenth century and received its official formula-
tion in the reformed breviary of Pope Pius V in 1568.*

The Magnificat: Mary's Prayer of Thanksgiving and Praise

My soul magnifies the Lord,
   and my spirit rejoices in God my Savior,
for he has looked with favor
   on the lowliness of his servant.
Surely from now on all generations
   will call me blessed;
for the Mighty One has done great things for me,
   and holy is his name.
His mercy is for those who fear him
   from generation to generation.
He has shown the strength of his arm;
   he has scattered the proud in the thoughts of their hearts.
He has brought down the powerful from their thrones,
   and has lifted up the lowly;
he has filled the hungry with good things
   and sent the rich away empty.
He has helped his servant Israel,
   in remembrance of his mercy,
according to the promise he made to our ancestors,
   to Abraham and his descendants forever.

The Angelus

V – The Angel of the Lord declared unto Mary.
R – And she conceived by the Holy Spirit.
Hail Mary … (Pray The Hail Mary here.)

V – Behold the handmaid of the Lord.
R – Be it done to me according your word.
Hail Mary …

V – And the Word was made Flesh.
R – And dwelt among us.
Hail Mary …

V – Pray for us, O Holy Mother of God.
R – That we may be made worthy of the promises of Christ.

LET US PRAY: Pour forth, we beseech you, O Lord, your grace into our hearts, that we to whom the incarnation of Christ, your Son, was made known by the message of an angel, may by his passion and cross be brought to the glory of his resurrection. Through the same Christ our Lord. Amen.

The Angelus originated with the eleventh-century monastic custom of reciting three Hail Marys at the Compline (Night Prayer) bell. The custom of reciting it in the morning grew from the monastic custom of saying three Hail Marys while the Prime (Morning Prayer) bell rang.[13]

Hail Holy Queen

Hail, holy Queen, mother of mercy,
our life, our sweetness and our hope.
To you do we cry, poor banished children of Eve.
To you do we send up our sighs,
mourning and weeping in this valley of tears.
Turn then, most gracious advocate,
your eyes of mercy toward us,
and after this our exile,
show unto us the blessed fruit of your womb, Jesus.
O clement, O loving, O sweet Virgin Mary!
Pray for us, O holy Mother of God, that we may be made worthy
of the promises of Christ. Amen.

*The current form of this prayer is from the Abbey of Cluny, France,
in the twelfth century.*

The Memorare

Remember, O most gracious Virgin Mary,
 that never was it known that anyone
who fled to your protection,
implored your help or sought your intercession,
was left unaided.
Inspired by this confidence,
I fly unto you, O Virgin of virgins my Mother;
to you do I come, before you I stand,
sinful and sorrowful;
O Mother of the Word Incarnate,
despise not my petitions,
but in your mercy hear and answer me. Amen.

The Memorare is a sixteenth-century version of a fifteenth-century prayer. Claude Bernard (1588-1641) popularized the claim that St. Bernard of Clairvaux (1090-1153) was the author of this prayer.

The Franciscan Crown

One of the most popular Franciscan prayers is the Franciscan Crown, a Franciscan Rosary of seven decades commemorating the Seven Joys of Mary:

1) The Annunciation,
2) The Visitation,
3) The Nativity,
4) The Adoration of the Magi,
5) The Finding of Jesus in the Temple,
6) The Resurrection,
7) The Assumption and Crowning of Mary

St. Francis of Assisi's Salutation to the Blessed Virgin Mary

Hail, my Lady, Holy Queen,
Mary, Mother of God.
You are the virgin made church
You have been chosen in heaven
by the most holy Father.
With his Most Holy Beloved Son and
the Holy Spirit he has consecrated you,
so that in you is all fullness of
grace and every good.

Hail, his palace, hail, His Tabernacle, his house.
Hail his vesture, hail his handmaid, his mother.
And, hail all you holy virtues who through
the grace and illumination of the Holy Spirit
are poured into the hearts of believers
so that you might transform unfaithfulness
into faithfulness to God. [14]

Saint Francis of Assisi's Prayer to the Virgin Mary

Holy Virgin Mary,
there is no one like you
among women.
Daughter and handmaid
of the Most High Sovereign King
and Father in heaven,
Mother of our Most Holy Lord Jesus Christ,
Spouse of the Holy Spirit,
pray for us
with Saint Michael the Archangel
 and with all the powers of the heavens
 and with all the saints
together with your most holy beloved Son,
Lord and Teacher.

—Office of the Passion[15]

Dante's Prayer to the Virgin Mother Mary

You, O Virgin Mother, daughter of your Son
Humble and high above all other creatures,
Your rank fixed by God's eternal plan,

You are the one who gave such nobility
To human nature, that its Creator
Did not disdain to make Himself its creature.

Within your womb love was rekindled
By the heat of which this flower has
Germinated in the eternal peace.

Here unto us you are a noonday torch
Of charity, and below among mortals
You are the living fountain-head of hope.

Lady, you are so great and so prevailing,
That we who wish grace, but don't run to
You, may long to fly, but have no wings.

Not only does your benignity give succor
To one who asks it, but oftentimes
Foreruns, of its own accord, the asking.

In you is compassion, in you is pity.
In you magnificence, in you unites
Whatever of goodness is in any creature.

Now does this man, who from the lowest
Depth of the universe even to here has seen
One after one the lives of souls,

Beg through your grace for the power
That with his eyes he may uplift himself
Higher towards the uttermost salvation.

And I, who never burned for my own seeing
More than I do for his, proffer all my prayers
To you, and pray they fall not short,

That you would scatter from him every cloud
Of his mortality so that with your prayers
The Highest Joy might be revealed to him.

Still further do I pray you, O Queen, who can do
Whatever you will, that after so great a vision, you
Keep him sound and persevering in his affections.

—Dante Alighieri, Secular Franciscan[16]

"Stabat Mater" of Franciscan Blessed Jacopone da Todi (1230-1306)

English Translation, Edward Caswall (1814-1878)

At the cross her station keeping,
Stood the mournful Mother weeping,
Close to Jesus to the last.

Through her heart, His sorrow sharing,
All His bitter anguish bearing,
Now at length the sword had passed.

Oh, how sad and sore distressed
Was that Mother highly blest,
Of the sole begotten One!

Christ above in torment hangs.
She beneath beholds the pangs
Of her dying glorious Son.

Is there one who would not weep,
Whelmed in miseries so deep,
Christ's dear Mother to behold?

Can the human heart refrain
From partaking in her pain,
In that Mother's pain untold?

Bruised, derided, cursed, defiled,
She beheld her tender Child,
All with bloody scourges rent.

For the sins of His own nation,
Saw Him hang in desolation
Till His spirit forth He sent.

O thou Mother: fount of love!
Touch my spirit from above,
Make my heart with thine accord.

Make me feel as thou hast felt;
Make my soul to glow and melt
With the love of Christ my Lord.

Holy Mother, pierce me through;
In my heart each wound renew
Of my Savior crucified.

Let me share with thee His pain,
Who for all my sins was slain,
Who for me in torment died.

Let me mingle tears with thee,
Mourning Him who mourned for me,
All the days that I may live.

By the Cross with thee to stay;
There with thee to weep and pray,
Is all I ask of thee to give.

Virgin of all virgins best,
Listen to my fond request:
Let me share thy grief divine.

Let me to my latest breath,
In my body bear the death
Of that dying Son of thine.

Wounded with His every wound,
Steep my soul till it hath swooned
In His very blood away.

Be to me, O Virgin, nigh,
Lest in flames I burn and die,
In His awful Judgment day.

Christ, when Thou shalt call me hence,
Be Thy Mother my defense,
Be Thy Cross my victory.

While my body here decays,
May my soul Thy goodness praise,
Safe in Paradise with Thee. Amen.

Notes

1. Bonaventure, *Major Life of St. Francis*, Translation and Introduction by Ewert Cousins (New York: Paulist, 1978), 199.

2. John Duns Scotus, *Parisiensia*, III, vii, 4, quoted in Mario M. DiCicco, OFM, *Gerard Manley Hopkins and the Mystery of Christ*, doctoral dissertation, Department of English, Case Western Reserve University, 1970, p. 36, footnote 1.

3. *The Sermons and Devotional Writings of Gerard Manley Hopkins*, ed. Christopher Devlin, S.J. (London: Oxford University Press, 1959), 197.

4. Alan Wolter, private document, "The Absolute Primacy of Christ." Cleveland, Ohio, (Mimeographed), quoted by DiCicco, 61-62.

5. *Through the Year with Francis of Assisi: Daily Meditations from His Words and Life*, Selected and translated by Murray Bodo. Cincinnati: St. Anthony Messenger Press, 1993), 95-96.

6. Celano, Second Life, 198, *Omnibus of Sources*, 521.

7. Author's translation. cf. Murray Bodo, *Through the Year with Francis of Assisi*, (Cincinnati: St. Anthony Messenger Press, 1993), 96.

8. Frances Teresa Downing, OSC, English translation and notes, *Saint Clare of Assisi, Volume One, The Original Writings* (Phoenix: Tau, 2012), Letter Three, 87.

9. Downing, Vol. 1, Letter Two, 53-55.

10. Downing, Vol. 1, Letter One, 35.

11. Eduardo Galeano, *Voices of Time: A Life in Stories* (New York: Picador/Henry Holt and Co., 2006), 2.

12. Ilia Delio, OSF, *Simply Bonaventure, 2nd Edition* (New York: New City Press of the Focolare, 2013), 86-87.

13. Herbert Thurston, "Angelus," *The Catholic Encyclopedia*, Vol. 1. (New York: Robert Appleton Co., 1907).

14. cf. Murray Bodo, *Through the Year with Francis of Assisi*, (New York, Doubleday and Co., 1987), 94.

15. *The Geste of the Great King / Office of the Passion of Francis of Assisi* (St. Bonaventure, NY: Franciscan Institute, 2001, reprinted by Tau Publications, Phoenix, AZ.)

16. Author's re-rendering based on the translation by Henry Wadsworth Longfellow of lines 1-36 from the "Paradiso" of *The Divine Comedy*, Canto XXX.

A Note from the Cover Artist

The painting on the cover is inspired by the work of Raphael, master painter of the Italian High Renaissance. In the fifteenth century, in Perugia—the very town where St. Francis experienced his formative imprisonment 300 years earlier—Raphael began painting Madonnas portrayed with serenity and gentleness. This painting style seemed fitting to adorn the cover of Fr. Murray's book. My personal approach in the studio has been to trust the creative process and allow the brush to guide my hand. The time in front of the canvas usually follows a period of Centering Prayer or Lectio Divina. I often listen to the rosary and contemplate the mysteries while I apply paint and wipe it away. Every time my painting completes itself, I feel more like a grateful witness to the creation of my work rather than the creator. This painting is no exception and the texture within the piece gives a hint of the mystery we experience when we, too, invite the Holy Spirit to overshadow us and our works both big and small.

—Holly Schapker
www.hollyschapker.com

Franciscan Media is a nonprofit ministry of the Franciscan Friars of St. John the Baptist Province. Through the publication of spiritual books, *St. Anthony Messenger* magazine, and online media properties such as *Saint of the Day, Minute Meditations,* and *Faith & Family,* Franciscan Media seeks to share God's love in the spirit of St. Francis of Assisi. For more information, to support us, and to purchase our products, visit franciscanmedia.org.

Live in love. Grow in faith.

MURRAY BODO, OFM, a Franciscan priest, is the award-winning author of numerous books, including the bestselling *Francis: The Journey and the Dream*, *Francis and Jesus*, *Mystics: Twelve Who Reveal God's Love*, nine books of poetry, and most recently *Surrounded by Love: Seven Teachings from Saint Francis*. Friar Murray has had his poems, stories and articles published in magazines and literary journals in the United States, England, and Ireland. He was a founding staff member of the Franciscan Pilgrimages Program and has led yearly pilgrimages in Assisi and the surrounding areas for over forty years. He resides in Cincinnati, Ohio.